The Predictable Profits Playbook:

The Entrepreneur's Guide to Dominating
Any Market—and Staying on Top

by

Charles E. Gaudet II

TELEMACHUS PRESS

Cover designed by Telemachus Press, LLC

Cover art:
Copyright ©
iStockphoto_000022015252/Maxiphoto
iStockphoto_000021133059/prapassong

Published by Telemachus Press, LLC
http://www.telemachuspress.com

Visit the author website:
http://www.PredictableProfits.com

ISBN: 978-1-940745-15-2 (eBook)
ISBN: 978-1-940745-16-9 (Paperback)
ISBN: 978-1-940745-90-9 (Hardcover)

Version 2014.04.17

Printed in the United States of America

10 9 8 7 6 5 4 3 2 1

Dedication

To the Entrepreneur who refuses to believe anything is "impossible."

*And to my wife Heather and our children Branson, Sage,
and Sabrina, who hold me accountable to my dreams.*

Contents

The Predictable Profits Playbook:

The Entrepreneur's Guide to Dominating Any Market—and Staying on Top

SECTION I:
IMPORTANT! READ THIS FIRST

Introduction

NO DOUBT YOU'VE been told hard work is the key to success, right? Then how do you explain why one entrepreneur may struggle 80 hours a week and only make half as much as another who works no more than 40 hours?

What's the difference between the local shoe store that barely makes six figures a year and the billion-dollar behemoth Zappos? After all, Nike footwear is Nike footwear no matter where you buy it.

How does a man living in a stark, 400-square-foot apartment—reduced to cooking his meals on a hotplate and washing dishes in a bathtub—create an organization that has generated hundreds of millions of dollars? (Tony Robbins, leading personal-growth expert)

Or how does another guy, growing up poor in the projects of Canarsie, Brooklyn and desperate to surpass the lifestyle of his truck-driving father, create a worldwide phenomenon and amass an estimated net worth of $1.1 billion?[1] (Howard Schultz, CEO of Starbucks)

You can see my dilemma. While I didn't grow up with a silver spoon in my mouth, I definitely wasn't destitute. I did what all American children are told to do: went to school, got good grades, and even graduated from the number one college in entrepreneurship[2], Babson College. In fact, I've been an entrepreneur since I was four (selling artwork to my neighbors) and

---

[1] http://en.wikipedia.org/wiki/Howard_Schultz
[2] Ranked #1 for Entrepreneurship by *U.S. News & World Report* 2013 "America's Best Colleges" for the 17th consecutive time.

can honestly say for the majority of my life, I've worked hard. For years, I'd set my alarm at 3:30 a.m. so I wouldn't "oversleep" and work until late evening. I didn't discriminate which days I worked—holidays and weekends didn't slow me down.

I thought I was doing everything right. But then why was it so damn hard for me to shatter the glass ceiling I was running up against to build the multimillion-dollar business I knew I could (and eventually did) create?

What was the real secret to those success stories I'd heard in the media? What did they know that I didn't?

Finding the answer became my obsession.

Tony Robbins once told me, "Success leaves clues." So I took it upon myself to look for the clues those successful entrepreneurs and organizations had in common.

This statement rings true for me: *"Entrepreneurship is doing the things most people won't, so you can spend the rest of your life like most people can't."*

Look, entrepreneurship isn't a walk in the park. But I hope this book gets to you before you find yourself in millions of dollars of debt, admitted to the emergency room for stress, and riddled with insomnia. (Oh, the joys of my life as an early entrepreneur!)

Yes, you're about to learn a better way.

About eight years ago, I made a discovery that profoundly changed my view about how companies grow. As it turns out, burning the midnight oil and traditional education doesn't differentiate those entrepreneurs who struggle to compete from those who have skyrocketed their businesses to market dominance.

Lo-and-behold, nearly every powerful organization—whether it's Apple or Nordstrom or Zappos or Disney—followed (and continues to follow) a stunningly similar formula. And it's the complete opposite of how most entrepreneurs think. My discovery (finally) explained why some businesses find growth opportunities in any economic situation while most cannot.

I pulled together the similarities needed to grow great companies and created a methodology. Once you see it, you'll understand how (embarrassingly) obvious the formula is. I call this methodology *Predictable Profits*.

Average entrepreneurs rely on one or two ways to grow their businesses: e.g., word of mouth, search engine optimization, pay-per-click advertisements, or even direct mail. Years ago, the Yellow Pages was the gold standard of advertising; the company with the most compelling ad in a category supposedly won the most business. The Yellow Pages was a tried and true strategy of most successful small businesses … and sometimes the only strategy they employed.

But now here's the difference of those I call *Strategic Entrepreneurs*. As one of my mentors eloquently put it: "If you want to play with the big dogs, you've got to stop pissing like a puppy!" That means if you want to grow your business into a multimillion-dollar organization, you must start thinking like the owner of a multimillion-dollar organization. Fortunately, with technological advances, you have many tools[3]—beyond the Yellow Pages—that level the playing field without needing the big advertising budget that was once required.

Multimillion-dollar businesses using the *Predictable Profits Playbook* take a different approach. They don't rely on one or two strategies; they make it a priority to create a *multitude* of strategies. A *fortress* of strategies! Here are a few:

- They nurture their leads and focus on building the relationships with their new customers.
- They capitalize on marketing strategies to get their best customers to eagerly come back and spend more money with them.
- They look at leveraging the media to establish authority, generate thousands (even millions) in free publicity and position themselves in their prospects' minds as the obvious choice.
- They focus not only on profits but on a mindset of creating a greater advantage and greater benefit for their customers to deliver a better result.

---

[3] I have compiled a list of resources for you at http://www.PredictableProfitsPlaybook.com

And these examples are only scratching the surface! But before we go on … if you take one thing from this book, consider this next point as the most important.

To borrow an analogy from Dan Sullivan, founder of Strategic Coach, *you want to imagine the growth of your company—the point of success—as getting to the boiling point.* If you've ever watched water boil, it starts with one bubble, then another and another. Then a series of small bubbles come together to form bigger bubbles until water reaches the boiling point.

Similarly, the strategies, ideas, and techniques you'll learn from this playbook can't be automatically implemented in their entirety overnight. (Rome wasn't built in a day, right?)

But each strategy you implement forms a metaphorical bubble in your pot. Then, as you implement another strategy, you form another bubble and another and another. Collectively, those small bubbles start to form bigger bubbles and before you know it, you're blasting down the rails of the growth track. You're dominating your market while out-earning, out-thinking, and out-competing your competition.

So fasten your seatbelts; you're about to enter a new world of opportunity and possibility. Ready? Hold on tight and let's get started.

Chapter 1:
The Incredible Opportunity
of a Down Economy

"The best way to predict your future is to create it."
—Peter F. Drucker, Management Consultant

I *COULD* TELL you that running a business is easy, but I won't. Enough millionaire and billionaire entrepreneurs would call my bluff. They know, as I do, that running a business has always been hard work. Most of the time, it's *extremely* hard work, whether it's a sole proprietorship or a firm with multimillion-dollar revenues employing a large staff.

According to the Small Business Administration, 50 percent of entrepreneurial ventures fail within five years—and the trend is worsening. The recent recession has put the clamp on consumer spending and capital; what's more, there may be no end in sight to these leaner times. Noted marketing author Seth Godin has argued that we're in a "forever recession" caused by an ongoing transition from an industrial-based economy to one driven by technology and globalization.[4]

---

[4] Godin, S. "The Forever Recession (And the Coming Revolution)." Seth Godin's blog. 2011.

Not only has the economy become more challenging for the average entrepreneur, but consumers today are far more selective and discerning than ever before. According to Google's handbook on online marketing, *ZMOT: Ways to Win Shoppers at the Zero Moment of Truth*, the average number of information sources used by shoppers DOUBLED in just one short year.[5] Plus three major developments have upped the ante: 1) the volume of information on the quality of products and services available; 2) the access consumers have to data for quick comparisons; and 3) a much wider range of competitors selling online.

The New Consumers will not spend money until they find a product or service that offers the best possible value and experience. They demand better service, want more choices and customization options, and insist on guarantees. They do their homework by researching a product and business on the Internet and through word-of-mouth recommendations.

Brink of Failure

Millions of average entrepreneurs finding themselves on the brink of failure are increasingly frustrated. Nothing they're doing seems to work. How do I know? Since the economic crash of 2008, I've received calls and emails from many struggling business owners. Most often, they feel overwhelmed and battered by the economy, a strong competitor, or both. They're sick of fighting price wars and are frustrated by competitors offering bait-and-switch deals. They're tired of wrestling dishonest vendors and wasting time and money on advertising that fails to deliver results. In addition, they continually have to cope with the stress of finding new customers or clients, they aren't getting enough repeat business, and their profits are paper-thin.

Hope in Spite of It All

Yet, within all this turmoil, certain entrepreneurs are strategically

---

[5] Google. ZMOT: *Ways to Win Shoppers at the Zero Moment of Truth Handbook.* 2012.

discovering ways to make profits, defying the harsh economic environment. Here's an example:

The setting: *We're in the midst of an economic environment demanding that entrepreneurs need to lower their prices to compete.*

The question: *Could a company succeed in selling a competitive product for 10 to 20 times more than their closest competitors?*

If you live near Lancaster, Pennsylvania, stop in at Gardner's Mattress & More, a small independent store, and talk to co-owners Ben McClure and Jeff Giagnocavo. These two entrepreneurs make four to five times more money on each sale than the industry average. "While the average ticket in the industry is about $500," McClure says, "we're averaging $2,000 and higher; up to $5,000 and $10,000-plus per ticket."

McClure also says his store is seeing:

- More customer leads,
- A significantly higher closing ratio, and
- More earnings per sale than competitors.

Plus their store just started selling a Swedish mattress brand ranging in price from $10,000 to $35,000. While their competitors—chains and smaller stores alike—compete on price and volume, McClure expects this high-end brand to be a significant area of growth for the business.

A truly amazing fact: McClure and Giagnocavo have accomplished their success within two years of taking ownership of Gardner's Mattress & More in 2010 *in the heart of the economic downturn.* Here's what McClure says:

"When things slowed down due to the economy, we realized the people who have a physical need for the products we carry found a way to invest in a better night's sleep through a new mattress. The slow economy didn't matter compared to the pain they felt while sleeping. People did, in fact, spend money in a down economy if it improved their health and well-being. Whatever business we lost by focusing on higher-end customers consisted of lower-end price shoppers—though we do have mattresses at a wide range of price points."

Many of us have had moments in our businesses when we've felt overwhelmed and helpless in the face of forces seemingly beyond our control. A downturn in the economy can cause incredible anxiety, fear, and frustration. However, as McClure and Giagnocavo have shown, it doesn't have to be that way. Their success is no fluke. Local and regional companies in a range of industries are making significant gains and dominating their markets. In some cases, they're even beating large national chains and conglomerates.

You'll meet many entrepreneurs like these throughout this book and learn how you, too, can get better at beating the Walmarts of the world—without competing on price or sacrificing your commitment to your product and customers or clients.

~~~~

"You are what you charge for. If you charge for undifferentiated stuff, you're in the commodity business. If companies, because of this recession, treat their offerings as just stuff, then they're commoditizing themselves."

—Joe Pine and Jim Gilmore,
authors of *The Experience Economy*

~~~~

The Right Strategies

Succeeding in a down economy requires the right skills and temperament—core values of my marketing coaching and consulting company Predictable Profits.[6] And my company has witnessed example after example. During what many economists called the worst economic period since the Great Depression, many of my clients grew their businesses by 30 to 50 percent—and some a lot more. This often happens within a few months of starting to work with the principles I teach throughout this book. I've also helped my clients hone in on their ideal customers and clients—those who will make them the most profits. This, in turn, enables them to cut back on the hours they're working by working smarter, not longer.

---

[6] Obtain free marketing tips and advice on my blog at http://www.PredictableProfits.com.

For example, one client had a database of 50,000 inactive leads she believed weren't buying simply because they weren't interested. With only two strategic emails to those on her database, she was able to generate a 100 percent increase in sales. Another client's business was suffering from a 35 to 50 percent merchandise return rate. Taking my advice, he was able to quickly reduce that rate to less than 2 percent while also increasing his sales by 35 percent. A third client—unknown among the lucrative client base he sought—today has industry celebrities knocking down his door. He generated just over $1.1 million in sales in 10 days using one of my strategies.[7]

Predictable Profits Results

Why do these strategies produce results like this? In part because I've spent the last decade identifying the common nuances that separate successful entrepreneurs such as McClure and Giagnocavo from the struggling entrepreneurs they compete against. I've poured nothing shy of 7,500 hours into understanding the breakthrough successes of some of the most innovative and respected entrepreneurs of all time—people such as Sir Richard Branson, Andrew Carnegie, Steve Jobs, Tony Hsieh, Jeff Bezos, Howard Shultz, Fred Smith, Walt Disney, and others. Plus I've spent the better part of my lifetime as an entrepreneur myself. In 2000, at age 22, I started a pet health insurance company and it earned a nomination by Ernst & Young as "One of the Nation's Best Seed-Stage Companies." When I was 24, I founded my first multimillion-dollar company and became a successful real-estate developer. Later, I founded a proprietary stock-trading company and investors across the globe sought my help to improve their own stock trading.

In addition, I traveled with Tony Robbins for a year and a half. Since that time, my wife and I have invested more than $500,000 to learn from highly successful people, including business leaders, authors, celebrities, and

---

[7] The government requires I tell you these results aren't typical and the examples I provide are extraordinary and the result of lots of hard work. While it's true that nothing is guaranteed, I've seen a correctly executed strategy produce wonders.

political leaders. I've been mentored by Marshall Thurber (who also taught Tony Robbins), Dr. John DeMartini, Dan Sullivan, and several others.

Based on my research and hands-on experience, I formulated and fine-tuned the simple, often counterintuitive, and highly powerful marketing methodology and strategies you'll discover in this book. This approach will enable you to do the following:

- Succeed in a down economy.
- Become the preferred provider sought by the best customers.
- Swipe market share from your competitors.
- Increase margins while growing demand.
- Multiply your prospect-to-sales ratio.
- Boost customer loyalty and build a raving fan base.
- Create predictable and rising profits from one month to the next.

The Predictable Profits methodology avoids gimmicks, schemes, and stunts. In fact, such tricks are adamantly opposed. Nor does this methodology require increased spending on marketing and advertising; in fact, much of it focuses on optimizing the marketing dollars you're already spending. It also flat-out rejects the most common techniques used to boost sales, insisting that business owners do not:

- Cut prices,
- Cheapen products,
- Rerun old deals,
- Push the same advertising, or
- Focus only on getting new customers while ignoring current customers.

Against the Flow but in the Know

I'm not alone in believing that most people are capable of going against conventional wisdom and achieving the exceptional. I learned this by following the remarkable insights of Sir Richard Branson, a man I admire so much I named my son after him.

What has made the difference for Branson? He's always been willing to challenge convention and provide greater value to those he seeks to serve. More than a flashy show, his Virgin brand consistently delivers the greatest value and experience it can. Branson has declared, "I can honestly say that I have never gone into any business purely to make money. If that is *your* sole motive, then I believe you are better off not doing it."

Fulfilling Needs by Bucking Convention

We are entrepreneurs in large part because we get a thrill out of fulfilling our customers' or clients' needs and making them happy. Not only that, we enjoy them appreciating the quality of our offerings. And when they do, they're a marketing force more powerful than any money can buy.

How did McClure and Giagnocavo build such a successful mattress business that their customers actively promote? They had the foresight and courage to buck convention as they:

- Targeted higher-end customers, while still offering products that serve a wide range of price points and brands.
- Positioned themselves as the trusted advisors on sleep by solving their customers' sleep problems with mattresses that address their sleep needs.
- Paid significant attention to offering the best overall customer service and experience.
- Built strong, lasting relationships with customers.
- Offered one of the best guarantees in the mattress business.
- Didn't compete on price or resort to gimmicks and ploys.

Gardner's Mattress & More exemplifies the incredible results that can be realized following the Predictable Profits methodology. Throughout this book, you'll meet more entrepreneurs like Ben McClure and Jeff Giagnocavo. Some of them have generated great success with the Predictable Profits methodology specifically, while others have implemented one or more of these methodologies on their own. All of them have built hugely successful businesses known for excellence.

Predictable Profits Philosophy and Methodologies

The core philosophy of the Predictable Profits methodology is this: stop competing on price. Instead, focus on increasing both margins and demand by delivering more value to your customers. Become known as a business of excellence.

The core practices for the Predictable Profits methodology are:

POSITIONING

- Identify a specific target market of preferred customers and focus on their needs rather than attempting to appeal to everyone.
- Identify and leverage a unique advantage point (UAP) that clearly distinguishes you from your competitors.
- Distinguish yourself as a trusted advisor in your market to both establish your authority and garner media coverage that's more powerful than advertising.
- Strengthen your relationships with prospects to vastly improve your conversion rate.

PRODUCT

- Continually improve your value proposition, always asking The Growth Factor™ question: "What else can I do for my clients or customers that will give them greater value?"[8]
- Create price elasticity among buyers to grow your price point, increasing your prices even as you increase demand.

---

[8] You can download a FREE Special Report on *The Growth Factor* at http://www.PredictableProfitsPlaybook.com

PROMOTION

- Create multiple pillars of income and revenue-generating opportunities.
- Build enduring relationships with customers or clients through the Three Phases of Marketing: Dating, Engagement, and Marriage.
- In the *dating* phase, maximize the power of direct response marketing and lead-generation strategies to create leads that become sales. Start a relationship.
- In the *engagement* phase, be a customer service over-achiever, following up after purchases to confirm satisfaction. Make special offers. Surprise customers with the unexpected.
- In the *marriage* phase, build on the trust you've established. Create a marketing multiplier effect. Provide preferred customers with early offers, extra information, and complimentary services. Customize communications to them, sending newsletters and congratulatory notes, and asking for their feedback. Conduct strategic up-selling and cross-selling.

I've seen this formula work for hundreds of businesses with a B2B (business-to-business) focus as well as a B2C (business-to-consumer) market. It's important to emphasize that the Predictable Profits methodology works for any kind of business, regardless of its size or sector.

Whether your company is business to business (B2B) or business to consumer (B2C), you're dealing with people who buy on emotion and rationalize with logic. It doesn't matter if you own an enterprise like Microsoft or the small doughnut shop on the corner; the underlying principles are the same.

Basketball legend Michael Jordan once said, "Some people want it to happen, some wish it would happen, others make it happen." With this playbook, I'm giving you the rules of the game, putting the ball in your court, and providing you with insights from the most elite business players.

Do you have the hunger to achieve more, the perseverance to run through any walls standing in your way, and the heart to win? If so, this methodology will place your business on the bullet train to success. Let's get started!

SECTION II:
POSITIONING YOUR
BUSINESS FOR PROFIT

Chapter 2:
Look Comprehensively, Act Specifically

"Power Principle: Know Your Niche! You will never appeal to everybody."
—Jay Abraham, CEO of the
Abraham Group, Inc.

IN THE MARKETING world, there's a popular saying: "The riches are in the niches." Gurus argue entrepreneurs must maintain a narrow and clearly defined focus. While there is validity to this statement, it's only the partial truth. Without the full story, entrepreneurs embracing this incomplete advice risk following the same dreadful fate as Palm, Borders, Blockbuster, Circuit City, Compaq and countless others. Yet without niching, your power, influence and income will be diluted like a teardrop in an ocean.

Though 'the riches *are* in the niches,' we need to first reveal the whole truth.

Years ago, I made the decision to wrestle (like the Olympians do ... not like the Hulkster). I learned quickly that if I wanted to be the best, I couldn't just be strong all around ... in addition, I needed to completely master a single move. Soon I was quickly and frequently dominating my competitors with the fireman's carry. Throughout my senior year, the fireman's carry was the primary strategy in yielding an undefeated record. Then

I got to the semi-finals of the state championship and, suddenly, my fireman's carry wouldn't work. My competitor had focused and trained on evading my strategic move. At this point, most people would continue with this one move because "it worked" and they would fool themselves into believing nothing else. Fortunately, I had a good coach who forced me to broaden my perspective and I won one of the most important matches of my career with a single-leg takedown (not the fireman's carry). Why do I share this story? Because the trap of niching is becoming so tightly engrossed and focused that the business fails to be observant and predictive of market and consumer changes. The riches *are* in the niches, but the businesses that succeed in tapping this wealth have a pulse on the market that borders obsessive.

Buckminster Fuller, visionary and author, talked about *The Great Pirates,* who at one point, were the most powerful men on the planet. They controlled the vast sea routes and eventually ruled the world. Fuller maintained that these pirates created countries and installed kings as their 'lieutenants' into the lands they controlled. The pirates felt their most significant threat was intelligence, so they demanded that the kings have all the bright people 'specialize' in a particular facet of life. The pirates ordered the kings to tell the people: '… each of you must mind your own business or off go your heads. I'm the only one who minds everybody's business.' This is how schools and our current form of education began. The commoners received specialized knowledge while *The Great Pirates* (known as today's top businessmen) retained comprehensive knowledge.[9]

The king was the only one who had a comprehensive view of everything in his land and reaped the benefits of the power derived from his specialized subjects. So how do you utilize niching without specializing? The misconception of only being a 'specialist,' with a sole focus on your niche, weakens your power and ability to compete. The trick is to be both the specialist and the king simultaneously. To have the focus of paring down your marketplace to find an abundance of wealth within a particular niche while

[9] Magic Without Cards. "The Great Pirate Bucky." 2010. [Available from: http://mediaecologist.blogspot.com/2010/04/great-pirate-bucky.html]

also constantly monitoring your entire market to be aware of fluctuations and adapt proactively, not reactively.

Marshall Thurber, a visionary and world-renowned business strategist, argues that entrepreneurs must look comprehensively at the bigger picture, while niching down to act specifically. You need to have a big picture view but take action inside of a narrowly defined and focused niche.

Thurber analogizes the specialization/niching dilemma with LASIK eye surgery. To achieve 'perfect vision,' one eye must be corrected to focus on *distance* while the other eye is focused on *near* vision. Businesses must focus both near (niching) and far (market) if they wish to see the picture of their company's success clearly. Companies maintaining such a tightly narrowed focus on their niche neglect to see changes in the competitive landscape around them and fail to adapt. Case in point, Borders bookstore didn't foresee the rise of e-books like Amazon and Barnes & Noble until it was too late. The company was convinced that having a great physical location with a cool café was enough to succeed. Sure, creating a niche for a physical bookstore worked for a while—but they took their eye off the bigger picture and didn't notice that the competitive landscape had changed until it was too late. This is why Thurber insists: "you must use <u>both</u> eyes."

This comprehensive view is further explained in a strategy called *The Grow Factor* (Chapter 5) and a more detailed report can be downloaded for free at http://www.PredictableProfitsPlaybook.com.

~~~~

"Look comprehensively and act specifically."
—Marshall Thurber, author and visionary

~~~~

"The Riches Are in the Niches"

I had a client who is perhaps one of the most talented competitors in the financial services industry. Bright and endlessly energetic, he's an incredibly gifted educator about trading practices. He offers a valuable set of products and services designed to help traders get better at what they do.

When we first started working together, I asked him to explain his offerings and their unique advantage. His answer was clear and succinct; I felt I'd gained quite a good understanding in a relatively brief time. Then I asked, "Who are your target clients?"

"Everybody," he replied.

When I asked him to be more specific, he said, "Look, I don't know of any mentoring program that's more complete or better than the one I offer my students. If they're trading Forex (Foreign Exchange Markets), E-Mini Futures, options, or stocks, I know I can help them. So as far as 'Who my market is,' I'd have to say it's anyone who trades any of those financial instruments. And if they aren't doing so, they should be, and they should be my client." I thought for a moment, then commented, "This is right off the page of Claude Hopkins's book *Scientific Advertising*, written in 1923. Hopkins said, 'If you try to talk to everybody, you talk to no one.'"[10]

Then I suggested we run a new campaign, focusing on a niche of traders who were most hungry, most in pain, and therefore, most likely to purchase his products immediately. As a result, I designed and conducted a launch for his company with a conversion rate beyond what conventional methods could have produced. He made a high six-figure income in the first few days and many millions in the months that followed.[11]

Those results can be largely attributed to narrowing his niche to his ripest market. One of his customers reached out to say, "Wow! When I saw your marketing material, I actually thought you were telling my story."

~~~~

"Consumers are more individualized than ever, expecting every good, service and experience to be addressing their unique and oh so important selves. Gone are the traditional demographic segments, the distinct consumer classes: this is all about being MASTERS OF THE YOUNIVERSE. Gone

---

[10] Claude Hopkins was one of the most transformational thought leaders in Direct Response Marketing. Anyone serious about Direct Response has read—or should have read—his book *Scientific Advertising* at least 10 times.

[11] Details behind strategies like this are also revealed inside of the Predictable Profits Insiders' Club. Go to http://www.PredictableProfitsInsidersClub.com for more information.

*too are the days when, as BusinessWeek so eloquently put it; 'the ideal was
not merely to keep up with the Joneses, but to be the Joneses.'"*[12]

—TrendWatching

~~~~

Define and Serve Your Niche

Most entrepreneurs miss the boat when they design a product, service, or
business they love *if they're not clear on exactly whose life they want to change.* You
need to know precisely who your niche customers are; this knowledge will
tell you how to both reach them and speak with them.

Potential buyers come to you with *their* unique situations. The more
closely you can identify with their problems—letting them know you genuinely understand their fears, frustrations, wants, and desires—the more
likely they'll put their faith and trust in you.

~~~~

*"Narrowing the focus on potential buyers allows specialized businesses to im-
plement marketing plans that highlight areas of a product that will appeal
most to a certain demographic. Marketing strategies can be tailored to the
specific product or service offered, creating a more effective overall advertising
campaign. Having a specialized business also makes it easier to pinpoint the
target audience."*[13]

—D.M. Clare Archer

~~~

The key is to not be all things to all people. Rather, be a critical solution provider to a specific set of people. You always want to seek the nexus
of peak profitability and customer enthusiasm for your offering. That requires finding the point at which you gain the highest margin while not

---

[12] TrendWatching. "Nouveau Niche Part 1." 2011. [Available from:
http://www.trendwatching.com/trends/nouveau_niche.htm]

[13] Clare Archer, D.M. "The Advantages of Niche Companies in Marketing." 2012. [Available
from: http://smallbusiness.chron.com/advantages-niche-companies-marketing-25788.html]

diminishing customer interest in your product or service. Then by speaking to and connecting with their pain, you'll be able to:

- Make each dollar you spend on marketing and advertising more cost-effective by lowering the cost per lead and per sale.
- Dramatically increase your conversion rate and spend less time in the sales process.
- Grow your revenue per customer.
- Increase client/customer loyalty.
- Cut down on prospects whose only concern is cost so you don't compete on price.

This is especially true of the *New Consumers,* a trend defined as consumers who jump on the Internet to research, read reviews and seek validation before making a purchase. *New Consumers* aren't swayed by mass marketing or products with mass appeal. They want individualization, customization, and personalization. TrendWatching, an independent firm that monitors global trends, describes them as the "nouveau niche."

~~~~

"Consumers are also more experienced than ever. They expertly cut through the crap, ignore advertising, and know which quality and price levels are fair. They actively hunt for the best of the best, and the best of the best is often NOT mass. The only mass they're willing to put up with is the stuff they don't really care about and can get on the cheap at ... Walmart."[14]

—TrendWatching

~~~~

---

[14] TrendWatching. "Nouveau Niche Part 1." 2011. [Available from: http://www.trendwatching.com/trends/nouveau_niche.htm]

Charge More for Specialization

In a 2007 TED talk,[15] Malcolm Gladwell, author of *The Tipping Point* and *Blink,* notes that not long ago, if you wanted spaghetti sauce, your choices were limited to a basic red sauce. However, at one point manufacturers learned that if they offered a range of spaghetti sauces with varying flavor profiles, they could charge a bit more for that specialization. In addition, they could grow their market share by meeting these niche demands.

Similarly, I spoke with an entrepreneur in his mid-40s who's a body builder and personal trainer, helping people improve their muscle tone and fitness. He said he didn't understand how further niching in his line of business would work; he simply targets people who want to build muscle. I explained (and he agreed) that most body-building products are marketed to teens and adults in their 20s and 30s. Then we talked about his age and the ages of other body builders he knows. In less than five minutes of conversation, we discovered an untapped niche, where he had previously thought none existed. He admitted he would pay more money for a specialty product positioned for body builders who were 40 or older, believing that the product targeted to his age range would more uniquely meet his needs.

This is what niching is all about.

The Power of a Niche: Example

The remarkable power of identifying a solid market niche was illustrated by Marshall Thurber, the world-renowned visionary and business consultant we discussed earlier:

> *"A lawyer who owns a law firm in Chicago is a client of mine, and his firm was floundering like crazy. I told him he was working too hard to make money as an attorney, and he asked, 'What do you mean?'*
>
> *"So I met with his company and I looked at his whole value proposition and level of service. We discovered that many people who are getting older*

---

[15] "Malcolm Gladwell: Choice, happiness and spaghetti sauce." YouTube. [Available from: http://www.youtube.com/watch?v=iIiAAhUeR6Y]

have amassed wealth over a lifetime and want to know how to pass on their
financial legacy. These people need to know where to go to get help.

"We discussed elder care and dealing with people in transition. The firm's
motto was revised to center on offering a symphony of unique solutions to peo-
ple in transition. Now these attorneys are elder care specialists, and the firm's
business is off the hook."

In this case, the firm not only identified a hungry crowd but a
sustainable hungry crowd. Looking forward, the law firm can rely on the
looming wave of aging Baby Boomers—a group that will last for a fairly
long time. And, of course, an aging population will continue to grow.
(This chapter later addressed how specializing can lead to more
predictable profits.)

Narrowing the Focus

Mike Michalowicz, entrepreneur, lecturer, and author of *The Toilet Paper
Entrepreneur* and *The Pumpkin Plan*, explains how he narrowed the focus of
his business:

*"My first company was all about computer network integration, which is
a better way of saying that when your computer broke at your office, I was the
guy who'd come in and break it more, then charge you for it. That was me.*

*"Before long, I was trying to scale the business and couldn't. I was in the
money trap, and the only way I thought I could grow was by working harder
and putting in more hours.*

*"The breakthrough moment happened when I sat down and evaluated my
clients and I came to two realizations. First, I was servicing a huge range of
clients. My business was all over the place and I was in the mentality that
any client is a good client.*

*"Second, when I looked at the clients who were the most valuable and I
enjoyed working with the most, and for whom I seemed to offer the best solution, I saw some commonality. A few of them were in the financial services
industry.*

"I'm a big believer in 'birds of a feather flock together.' Once I discovered this niche in the financial services industry—primarily in hedge funds—I stopped running around knocking on doors and trying to get the next sale. Instead, I reduced the quantity of time I spent marketing and selling and concentrated on the hedge fund industry.

"Very quickly, my company name became recognized in the industry, and within one year, we were ranked in a hedge fund journal listing as one of the top three providers of integrated technologies for hedge funds. A year prior to that, we didn't even know what a hedge fund was.

"What this points to is that, if you focus, you can readily start learning where these clients congregate and can insert yourself where they gather. Selling involves less going out and drumming up more business. It's now a more concentrated effort."

Similarly, Siamak Taghaddos, cofounder of Grasshopper, which specializes in telecommunications for entrepreneurs, says:

"In terms of the product and being successful with it, it was about always being able to say 'no' in terms of helping everyone and making a product for everyone.

"In our space, some companies declare they're for the small business owner; but they also have VOIP hardware phone systems that no two- or three-person business would need, so they go for the mid-market. Those mid-market companies then need sales reps to sell their IT departments, and the business becomes a sales organization. Then they need venture capital to build out a full-fledged phone system.

"Not having a specific niche leads to making bad decisions and wrong investments. By understanding who your target is and never swaying from that unless you have to, you will make the most productive decisions to focus on serving the entrepreneurial market."

As this example shows, as you start and build a business, refrain from diverting your attention from your core competency. In politics, they call it "going off message." To succeed, be sure you keep "on message."

~~~~

"Instead of targeting millions to reach thousands, we now target thousands to reach millions."[16]

—Weber Shandwick

~~~~

Make More by Saying No at Times

For Ben McClure, co-owner of Gardner's Mattress & More, knowing his niche—people seeking to solve their sleep problems—helped him understand where his business was off message. In turn, this helped him understand how to properly recalibrate his product mix to better serve a lucrative niche. He says:

> *"When I took over the store, we always had carried bedroom furniture, youth furniture and bunk beds, futons, and other related bedroom furnishings. In many ways, we were all over the map from a selection standpoint. We had no clear message and not enough money to market all the categories of products.*
>
> *"So we dropped the bedroom categories from our product mix. This allowed us to display more unique mattress options to meet more of our customers' sleep needs. Instead of having a scattered marketing approach, our message is now laser-beam focused: It's on mattresses and the process by which to buy a mattress, as well as on solving our customers' sleep issues and alleviating their mattress-buying concerns.*
>
> *"No one else in our market has taken this approach, and identifying that was crucial to our current success. As a result, we actually have fewer staff on the floor than before but much higher closing ratios and more profitability."*

McClure is not only effectively differentiating his business; he's also growing his price point and making significantly more money on each sale.

Their experience shows the benefit of targeting your offerings and marketing to those who have the most pressing need for the highest quality

---

[16] Factbrowser.com. "Instead of targeting millions to reach thousands, we now target thousands to reach millions." 2010. [Available from: http://www.factbrowser.com/facts/453/]

of goods and services you can offer—and who will pay the best price. A basic tenet of capitalism is that high demand for a scarce or valuable resource leads to greater price mobility. Thus, consumers—especially *New Consumers*—will actually pay a premium for a product that uniquely solves their problem.

Offer Your Existing Product to Other Specific Markets

Some entrepreneurs say they've already created their product, it works for everyone, and it's been selling. But niching doesn't mean you have to design a new product. Instead, you target your offering to *specific* markets.

For example, I had a coaching call with a successful entrepreneur about a product that helps people improve their golf swing. Immediately, I suggested he could target it to specific populations of golfers. Younger guys want to hit it out of the park, while women might want to gain consistency with their game. Older players may be looking to improve accuracy and continue to advance their game as they get older. The fundamentals of the swing are the same, but he's essentially tailoring the same offering to niche populations.

~~~~

"'Customer density' can be achieved by collecting a small number of customers from each of many locations. The customer gets the benefit of dealing with a supplier who 'really knows and understands' the product category, and the retailer gains expertise from the simplicity of focus ... Specialization is not only possible but perhaps, from the customer's point of view, even preferable. More and more, we see the emergence of highly focused, single product category players gaining traction with consumers."[17]

—David Bell, Wharton School

~~~~

---

[17] David Bell, Xinmei Zhang, and Yongge Dai. "Wharton: Knowledge in Action: Thin-Slicing and Retailing on the Internet." 2012. [Available from: http://www.google.com/think/columns/thin-slicing-and-retailing-on-the-internet.html]

Avoid Difficult, Costly Clients

Take a moment to think about your best clients—those easiest and most satisfying to deal with and those who spend the most money with you. Depending on your business, I imagine you can easily come up with a list of five or 10 clients who meet this description.

Now, how valuable would it be to you if you could consistently duplicate them so your entire customer base consists of these ideal clients?

Correctly identifying your niche will not, in and of itself, replicate your best clients or eliminate your difficult, low-margin customers. That's only one piece to that puzzle. But by focusing on the right niche of those most "hungry" clients, you're honing in on the most likely group of people who find your products or services valuable.

The people in the right niche:

- Better appreciate the universe of benefits you provide and how these benefits serve their needs, and
- Enthusiastically embrace your offerings because they feel a true connection to you as a peer and the unique provider of the solution to their problem.

Michalowicz made exactly this discovery when he studied which clients were most satisfying to deal with, were happiest with their experience, *and* brought in the most revenue. As he worked through his client list, he had this valuable insight that he shares here:

"I sorted my clients first by revenue and determined who my biggest clients were. Then I sorted the list by how much I liked dealing with them, putting either a smiley face or a frowny face next to each. Then came the epiphany.

"I discovered the lowest-revenue clients had the most frowny faces. What's more, some of these clients did small projects with me and cost me an inordinate amount of time. Then they didn't pay me much for the work or would delay payments and so on. This reminded me of Pareto's Principle, or the eighty/twenty rule, in which twenty percent of your clients yield eighty percent of your revenue. The inverse of that is eighty percent of your clients yield only twenty percent of your revenue.

"Finally, I looked for commonalities among that desirable twenty percent. I noticed a concentration in the financial services industry. That told me where [my niche] hangs out and I started finding clones of my best clients. My business got huge."

As you dominate one niche, you can then seek out additional related niches for which your product would be useful. You'll likely have to adapt it to fully meet the needs of this niche and/or adjust the message behind your marketing. However, once you've mastered niching, you can incrementally expand your efforts without creating brand new products.

~~~~

"Within your niche market, you are seen as the only viable solution. You understand and articulate the market's needs, hopes, dreams, and problems better than anyone else, and you offer clear-cut solutions that your market will prize and desire exclusively from you."[18]

—Jay Abraham, CEO of the Abraham Group, Inc.

~~~~

Your desired result? To maximize the potential for your product or service. In part, you do this by having a comprehensive and big picture view while simultaneously finding the right niche, dominating it, and then expanding it—that is, reaching into new and related groups of people who are *hungry* for what you have to offer.

The next chapter emphasizes the importance of providing that special advantage that will help you dominate your niche.

---

[18] Abraham, J. *The Sticking Point Solution: 9 Ways to Move Your Business from Stagnation to Stunning Growth in Tough Economic Times.* 2009: Vanguard Press. P. 25.

Chapter 3:
Identifying Your Unique Advantage Point

"In the factory we make cosmetics; in the drugstore we sell hope."
—Charles Revson, founder of Revlon

MY FIRST QUESTION to any potential client is always, "What makes your business unique?" Surprisingly, many entrepreneurs don't know exactly what makes them stand out. They rattle off answers like better product, lower prices, higher quality service, and so on. These are all important attributes—except for low prices[19]—but they don't go far enough to differentiate and define the superior value of what's offered. They don't articulate a *Unique Advantage Point.* Nor do they reliably entice the *New Consumer.*

You may be familiar with the concept of a *Unique Selling Proposition* (USP)—the characteristic or component of your product that differentiates it from others in the same market. Instead, I prefer to talk about a *Unique Advantage Point* (UAP). This means you need to promote your business not only by differentiating it from competitors (unique), but by identifying a particular way in which your business is *superior* (advantage).

---

[19] Sir Richard Branson says competing on price in a world with so many large competitors is "like getting into a bleeding competition with a blood bank." [Available at: http://en.wikipedia.org/wiki/Strategic_entry_deterrence]

In other words, your *Unique Advantage Point* articulates and represents the one-of-a-kind benefits, value, experience, and advantage you offer each customer. It makes your business more compelling and special than the world of me-too competitors. The UAP reassures people that becoming *your* client all but guarantees they'll achieve the ultimate result they desire.

Provide Special Value Within Your Niche

The concept of a *Unique Advantage Point* is, in fact, unique to the Predictable Profits approach. Throughout this chapter, you'll meet entrepreneurs discussing their UAPs within the context of their USP. From there, your goal is create *your* most powerful Unique Advantage Point.

You may be wondering: Does my business *have* to be unique? Isn't that requiring a lot? Yes, but that's the point. If you craft a UAP for your clients, they will not only *want* to return to you but will *have* to return to you. Business growth expert Paul Lemberg stresses it this way:

> *"It's about finding something within you and your business that people want and delivering it as a distinctive package so that if they want your unique constellation of benefits, they have to get it from you."*

Talking Software to Bankers

One of Paul Lemberg's first businesses provides a great example. Although he was one of the first business coaches to hit the scene, he got his start by building his own successful companies. One of these was a software company offering a solution targeted to the financial services industry. The key to this early success, he emphasizes, was his ability to clearly differentiate his solution:

> *"My software company was successful not because we had any idea what we were doing in terms of running a business. We didn't. However, we made a lot of money because a) our product was unbelievable, and b) the particular gift I brought to the company was translating the technology into banker's speak. What the bankers hated more than anything was being talked down*

to by technology guys. They didn't understand technology at the time, and the technology guys had been doing it forever.

"So our real differentiation in the marketplace was helping them understand the technology and the ROI [Return on Investment] of our solution without making them feel they were being talked down to.

"I was able to break down the technological solution into a value proposition in a way nobody else was doing, and when I spoke with clients, they said, 'Oh, we can do that.'

"And when I specialized in working with software companies, I'd tell them, 'The reason you can't sell your product is because nobody understands the ROI. If they don't understand the ROI, they won't peel three-hundred thousand dollars out of their pockets and buy the product.'

"So I developed a method for articulating what the real value proposition is—and that was enormous."

Lemberg solved his clients' software problems and explained his *Unique Advantage Point* by saying, "They not only get excellent software that will generate a significant ROI, but when they work with my company, I help them understand and execute on that value."

Free Shipping Both Ways

Looking for an example of the difference between a *Unique Selling Proposition* and a *Unique Advantage Point?* Consider the edge Zappos offers in its terms and service.

This company has one of the largest online catalogs of shoes and clothing available. While that fact constitutes a good selling proposition, it doesn't go far enough. In addition, Zappos assumes all of the handling risk by offering free shipping and returns on products up to one year after purchase—much longer than most return policies. Plus, Zappos complements this policy with extraordinary customer service. In comparison to their competitors, this is a very substantial unique advantage.

Wiring Old Houses

Consider the *Unique Advantage Point* of my friend Nate Moss's electric business in Portsmouth, New Hampshire.

Moss does everything an electrician is supposed to do. He works long hours and provides the best possible service he can. Polite and efficient, he unfailingly delivers a high-quality job. However, you'd expect any electrician you'd hire to do that, wouldn't you?

Still, Moss sets himself apart by positioning his company as a specialist *in the wiring of old homes.* Anyone who owns an older home understands all too well the special, costly challenges involved in repair or renovation. They also tend to have strong emotional attachments to these houses. Moss promotes himself as an electrician who has a unique understanding of the building techniques of different eras. This approach allows him to achieve higher quality with finer detail that's consistent with historical standards, plus it requires fewer subcontractors to complement his work.

He has also conveyed to his customers that he shares their emotional attachment to these beautiful homes. This smart positioning has made him the top choice in a relatively wealthy niche market. It's allowed him to thrive even during one of the worst recessions in history—a time when people have pulled back significantly from investing in their homes. As he recounts:

> *"I started my business at the worst time possible. The economy had just tanked, the real-estate market was going down, and nothing was going right in 2008. However, this was something I'd been working toward for more than twenty years.*
>
> *"I did something differently, though. Living in New England, we're sur- rounded by old homes that tend to be owned by people looking for something special. I noticed a niche for this kind of work, so I positioned myself such that, if you had an old house, I was your guy. I even lettered my truck to say I specialize in old homes.*
>
> *"When I first started the business, I remember driving down the road and seeing this old lady in a nice Mercedes Benz writing down something from the side of my truck. I thought I either was about to get a new job or a nasty phone call for cutting somebody off.*
>
> *"It turned out she had a multimillion-dollar farmhouse she wanted re- wired soup to nuts. I got the job because of my tagline. I haven't worked fewer than six days a week since."*

Nutrition Bars for a Dancer's Body

In another great example of entrepreneurs fashioning a niche-related *Unique Advantage Point,* former ballet dancers Aaron Ingley and Julia Erickson co-founded Barre. This company produces a selection of high-quality nutrition bars to meet the needs of dancers.

As Erickson tells the story, she had given up buying so-called nutrition bars because they were loaded with sugar and didn't pack enough nutritional punch. More than that, they made her feel weighed down, and she worried about maintaining her dancer's physique. Then, while rehearsing for Swan Lake with the Pittsburgh Ballet Theatre, she wanted a snack that would be both convenient *and* nutritious. So she developed a nutritional bar mix based on her own need to maintain maximum energy for an extended time without weighing her down or affecting her slim appearance. What she created worked well and, before long, she was sharing her bars with other dancers. A pirouette or two later, Erickson and Ingley realized they had a marketable product on their hands.

At about the same time, Ingley retired from dancing to study for an undergraduate degree in management and history at the University of Pittsburgh. Armed with the right recipe and solid business knowledge, she and Erickson wanted to distinguish their business in a market inundated by nutrition bars. They turned to the origin of their product, as Erickson explains:

> *"The primary differentiator is that our bar was developed by me for my own needs as opposed to a product developed in a lab that someone decided to market to a certain sector. We came up with the tagline 'Developed by dancers, created for everyone.' We try to tell our story as authentically as possible: This is who we are, and I created this bar that's good and healthy, and I want to share it with you."*

Their brilliant emotional differentiator offers customers an "inside secret" so they can attain top athletic performance while remaining lean. As Erickson puts it:

> *"We try to hit an aspirational note. 'Listen, you can do this.' For dancers, our jobs depend on it, so take a sheet from our playbook."*

Their message is working. Ingley and Erickson recently made deals with the health food retailer Whole Foods and partnered with a distributor that focuses on natural and health food retail stores.

The Benefit of Emotional Connection

These successes—of Moss's electrical business, Zappos, and Ingley and Erickson's Barre bars—go beyond clearly differentiated value propositions. Each also tap an emotional connection with consumers. In this regard, Zappos overtly promises to deliver happiness. Moss shares the emotional attachment his customers have to their homes, and Ingley and Erickson hit one of the deepest emotional issues among consumers—the desire to be in good shape.

The driving motive of Charles Revson (Revlon Cosmetics)—*In the factory we make cosmetics; in the drugstore we sell hope*—also highlights an emotional connection. In one succinct yet compelling phrase, Revson captures why a young girl or woman would select his products from the rows of other cosmetics in a drugstore.

Remember Siamak Taghaddos, cofounder of Grasshopper, who offers a telecommunications service for entrepreneurs? How could his business possibly have emotional appeal? Well, Taghaddos sells something far more comprehensive than a virtual phone service. He promotes a solution that helps business owners experience their entrepreneurial dreams, which is captured in the phrase: *Sound Like a Fortune 500 Company.* As he notes:

> *"We really wanted to express that we stand for something in a way that's focused and creates an emotional impact. We match our brand with an aspirational message that entrepreneurs can connect with on a feeling level."*

The Value of a Powerful Tagline

Just as Charles Revson's powerful tagline helped establish one of the longest-running brands in the industry, successful companies can capture their unique constellation of benefits in a punchy summation. The best hit at an emotional level while conveying a solution to buyers. For example, FedEx used this: *When it absolutely, positively has to be there overnight.* L.L.Bean leads its marketing with a guarantee: *Shipped for free, guaranteed to last.* And Zappos: *Free shipping and free returns 365 days per year.* The powerful tagline for a landscaping business says *Beautiful landscaping completed on time, on-budget, and with your 100 percent satisfaction or you don't pay a single penny for our labor!* I love it!

In building my Predictable Profits Insiders' Club[20] where I reveal advanced strategies for growing your business, I use the tagline: *Business building strategies guaranteed to be worth over 100 times your investment into the club, or your money back.* When I tell a room full of entrepreneurs this is what I offer, believe me, they sit up and take notice.

I strongly encourage you to spend time crafting a quality tagline. Doing so will not only make your marketing more persuasive, but the process will help identify exactly what special advantage you want to offer.

Identifying Your Unique Advantage Point

To help business owners craft their unique offering, I suggest asking these simple but powerful questions:

> **Question 1:** What is the ultimate advantage, benefit, or result my prospects want to achieve?
> **Question 2:** How will my product/service make my clients' life better in a way that's not currently offered to them?
> **Question 3:** What makes my business better than my competition?

Siamak Taghaddos explains how he and his partner developed their company's *Unique Advantage Point*, a term he refers to as his "DNA":

---

[20] Get cutting-edge and advanced information to grow your business by becoming a member of the Predictable Profits Insiders Club at http://www.PredictableProfitsInsidersClub.com

"Think about what you have and offer that no one else can replicate. We did an exercise in which we supposed someone had an unlimited budget to start a Grasshopper-like service feature by feature, same exact everything. We then asked: What do we have that another person could never replicate? Responses included best support, uptime, service, people, etc. However, anyone with money can create those things. We realized the one thing that anyone with money could never replicate is our unique connection with entrepreneurs. Even in a commodity business, others can't replicate the founder's story and how we uniquely understand and solve a person's problem."

Your *Unique Advantage Point* must also address the pains and desires of your market. So after my clients have answered those first three questions, I help them further refine their unique advantage point by adding these questions:

Question 1: What are the most significant areas of pain, trouble, or worry in your market as they specifically relate to your product or service (e.g., what keeps your customers awake at night)?

Question 2: What would your ideal client say is missing from your competitors' offerings?

Question 3: What else can you do that will differentiate you from your competitors?

Question 4: If I spent five minutes with your ideal client, how would they describe the advantage of doing business with you that's unique from others?

Question 5: What is it about these advantages that would motivate someone to take action right away?

Working through these questions will give you remarkable clarity about what your market needs and desires, while suggesting how you can fulfill those needs and desires—in your unique way.[21]

---

[21] To create your own *Unique Advantage Point*, download the worksheet at http://www.PredictableProfitsPlaybook.com

Knowledge of Your Clients and Your Own Uniqueness

Taking an additional step, speak with your target customers as a way to research the problems they're dealing with. Be sure to find out their frustrations about other products or services available to them. As you get into these conversations, unanticipated questions will emerge. The following questions make a good start, so ask yourself first:

- How am I unique?
- Am I faster or do I offer quicker turnaround service than my competitors?
- Is my business safer than others in my industry or offer greater security?
- Am I the most trusted?
- Am I the most tested?
- Is my testing process unique?
- Is my product/service unique?
- Do I offer more support, education, or training than others?
- Am I the most fun to work with?
- What's unique about the experience I offer?
- What's unique about the guarantee I offer?
- Am I more convenient to deal with than others?
- Is there anything unique about the quality of my product?
- Are my results unique and better than the industry standard?

While getting to know your clients and their problems, you want to give them the opportunity to get to know you; after all, people do business with people they *know, like,* and *trust.* If you can make your business seem more *personal* and less like a faceless organization, you'll reap the benefits of a highly engaged relationship with your prospects.

Think about this: people who purchase Apple largely do so because Apple has a "personality." The company continued to show this personality with its "Apple versus PC" ads and infusing the likability of Steve Jobs.

Instead of being a big "faceless" corporation like other large computer companies, Apple took a different approach. Similarly, Progressive Insurance has built a *personality* around Flo; Geico around the gecko; and even Budweiser did so for a while with its "Whaaaatsuuup" commercials. The big guys do this for a reason; displaying personality works!

As a small business owner, this personality can be (and, in most cases, should be) you. That's the only reason why I make liberal use of photographs and divulge personal (sometimes embarrassing) stories of myself on my blog and elsewhere. It humanizes my business and opens the door for my followers to have a relationship with my company and me.

The Power of Adding Personality to Your Business

You've met Mike Michalowicz, noted business consultant, lecturer, and author of *The Toilet Paper Entrepreneur* and *The Pumpkin Plan*. He made his first big breakthrough as an entrepreneur with his computer network integration company. That kind of business may seem as technical and dry as they come, but that's one reason Michalowicz allowed himself to express his distinctive personality while reaching out to his target customers. He claims doing this significantly factored into his company's success:

> *"What we did was fairly straightforward—computer networks. But we specifically did them for hedge funds, taking the time to speak with hedge fund managers so we could learn about their unique technical requirements. This enabled our service to provide a level of customization that held considerable value for them.*
>
> *"The other component, while less quantitative, is maybe more significant. It was our style. I exploited my natural tendencies. In high school, I was the class clown and shunned by the teachers because I disrupted the class with my self-deprecating style of humor. So I applied that to my business. While creating computer networks for hedge fund companies, we had fun, and our clients would see that. We weren't goofs or disruptive to their business, but when our guys came out, clients wanted to hang out and joke with them.*
>
> *"Behind the scenes, our business culture developed that sense of fun, too. At the end of each week, we gave out the F-Up Award. All ten of us would sit down and ask who made the biggest, dumbest mistake that week.*

Sometimes crazy things would come up. Whoever got the trophy had to carry it around the next week, no matter where he went, even to client appointments.

"And you had to add something to the trophy, so after a year or two of doing this, fifty or sixty items had been added to this trophy. It was like a homeless man's shopping cart of stuff the winner had to carry around to clients.

"This distinguished the essence of who we were. We weren't only nerds; we were fun, goofy nerds who served hedge funds. This was all based on my natural, distinguishing flavor."

Michalowicz got to know the hedge fund world well enough to understand that his somewhat whacky personality would strike a positive cord there. However, that may not be appropriate for your market—or for you. The point is making yourself known as a *person* to your customers or clients. (The next chapter expands on the ways you can develop a reputation and relationship with customers to make them *yours*.)

How do you want to show up to your customers? How do you want them to view you? If you look at any of the Virgin brands, such as Virgin Airlines, the *personality* of the business aligns with the company's founder, Sir Richard Branson, a well-known "rebel" billionaire who likes to have a good time and push boundaries. Therefore, whether Branson is wearing a wedding dress or creating a humorous safety video for his airlines, he's blazing the path of a rebel by being different.

5 Deadly Sins of Crafting a Unique Advantage Point (UAP)

Let's briefly address the five deadly sins to avoid when crafting your *Unique Advantage Point*. I've seen many entrepreneurs fall into these traps.

Sin #1: Assuming that good service is a *Unique Advantage Point.* The *New Consumer* expects that you offer the best service possible and knows that every one of your competitors claims to offer the highest level of service, too. Therefore, promise of service is rarely enough on its own.

Exceptions to this rule exist, of course. Zappos, for example, offers a truly exceptional quality of service in an industry not known for service. Typically, online retailers make it difficult to return products and speak to a human; in fact, they outsource many customer support functions internationally. Zappos has turned all that on its head to create a *WOW!* experience.

Sin #2: Believing you're already unique. Too many business owners think they're already doing enough to stand out. But in none of our examples did the entrepreneurs sit back and hope that customers or clients would *recognize* what's unique about their offerings.

Many entrepreneurs fall into the trap of being so intimately tied to their product or service, they can't see things from the consumer's perspective. Always remember: What people in your market *recognize* about your business will only be a small fraction of what you're doing. They see the tip of the iceberg above the water, not all that's below it.

Be real. Your belief in your own superiority may not be well supported by what those in your target market see. To counter resistance on this point, ask these key questions:

- Do consumers in your market clearly view you as the obvious choice?
- If you polled your customers, would they uniformly describe your unique advantages without hesitation?
- Is your business growing or is it stuck?
- Do you ever feel forced to compete on price?

By responding to these questions, my clients recognize they could and should be doing more to establish their business as the obvious choice in their market.

Sin #3: Writing your UAP in stone. As time passes, the needs and demands of the market will evolve, so you must adapt accordingly.

Domino's Pizza failed to do this for a time until the company began to understand the need to shift. Domino's UAP was that customers would get a fresh, hot, delicious pizza delivered to their door in 30 minutes or less, or else it's free. That premise got the company off and running, but before long, competitors flooded the market with similar promises.[22]

Because Domino's was slow to recognize the changing competitive landscape, its advantage was watered down. It began to struggle, seeking ways to create new differentiators. One concept was the Pizza Tracker—an application that allows customers to track the progress of their delivery online. Another was to dramatically alter its pizza recipes after consumers gave them poor ratings. That response to consumer feedback helped reestablish Domino's as a unique pizza provider. Recently, the company has shown signs of rebounding.

As they grow their businesses and perhaps move into new markets, entrepreneurs can err by watering down what made their products or services unique. You don't want to lose that part of your company's DNA. Adapt and grow, yes, but dilute, never.

Sin #4: Being a copycat. This may seem blindingly obvious, but you'd be surprised how many people make this mistake. Take the case of Skechers and its Bob's shoe line—a blatant copy of Toms Shoes. Toms, which designs and sells a range of mostly casual shoes, has one of the better founding stories of recent years. It also has a powerful value proposition: With each pair of shoes Toms sells, the company donates a pair of shoes to a child in need. The company's DNA goes back to 2006 after Blake Mycoskie traveled to Argentina and witnessed the difficulties poor children faced there because many had no shoes. That distinctive, authentic, and emotionally compelling story became the foundation of Toms' success.

Skechers developed a nearly identical line of shoes with the same social mission as Toms. But the obvious copycatting was seen as a cynical marketing ploy and set off a firestorm of negative comments online within 24 hours. As FastCompany.com noted:

---

[22] The company also had a PR and branding problem after a couple of high-profile lawsuits that resulted from crashes involving its delivery drivers.

"Skechers not only showed a lack of creativity and originality, but they left themselves wide open to accusations of disingenuous social concern.

"This is a great example of where so many brands go wrong. Consumers do not respond to the 'how' of what you do but the 'why.' That's because the 'why' is emotional and something they can connect to. The 'how' is simply the expression of that emotion.

"Skechers would have done far better to copy Toms in a different way. Its leaders should have thought through what they stand for and then acted on that with equal generosity. Then their consumers would have a way to connect with the brand that warranted admiration."

Sin #5: Being purely logical. The Toms example emphasizes another important point: People buy largely on emotion, and secondarily on the rational logic of differences in offers. Too many companies rely too much on the logic side of the equation. Toms effectively speaks to people's emotions by authentically recounting Mycoskie's inspiration to provide a one-for-one model of giving shoes to children. As a result, the company can charge a considerable premium over comparable shoes.

In summary, you'll be more successful when you offer a *Unique Advantage Point* or UAP that sets you apart with a value-added tweak. If that touches the heart or tickles the funny bone or provides something no one else can legitimately copy, you'll draw consumers like bees to honey.

As the next chapter explains, you can enhance your success by approaching your sales from an advisory standpoint and giving advice customized to your niche.

Chapter 4:
Becoming the Obvious
Choice to Do Business With

"You want to be seen from now on by everyone you deal with as the definitive expert source and the most trusted advisor ... not as a purveyor of a commodity; not as a generic seller of services and products."

—Jay Abraham, CEO of the
Abraham Group

DONALD TRUMP WAS once paid $1.5 million for a single speaking engagement. [23] Imagine! People line up with their wallets open, begging him to speak in front of their audiences. But do you really believe Donald Trump is the most intelligent real estate guru or business owner? What about Dr. Phil, one of the most highly paid psychologists? Do you believe he's the best, most intelligent psychologist in the world? Yet Dr. Phil had an estimated $72 million in earnings as of June 2013 according to Forbes.[24] Heck, it was reported Kim Kardashian was paid $20,000 to tweet

---

[23] http://www.forbes.com/2008/03/18/trump-reagan-blair-biz-media-cx_lh_0318speeches.html

[24] http://www.forbes.com/profile/dr-phil-mcgraw/

a product endorsement on her Twitter account and earned $50,000 to $100,000 per event to appear at clubs, parties, and other events.[25]

How are they able to do this? It's because they have "names" that people in their target market know and respond to. They leverage their industry celebrity status to generate a predictable, consistent stream of profits. As a trusted authority, people seek you out and opportunities come to you. You don't have to be the "best" or the most successful; you simply have to know how to position yourself in the minds of your market as an expert.

~~~~

"As a main street retailer you are not competing against the Walmarts of the world on the basis of content, and certainly not on selection or price. What you are competing on is that you are the trusted advisor."
—Paul Lemberg, author and entrepreneur

~~~~

Just look at a few examples of these industry authorities who've solidified themselves as experts in their market:

- In home comforts, it's Martha Stewart.
- In advertising, it's Donny Deutsch.
- In business management, it's Peter Drucker.
- In personal development, it's Tony Robbins.
- In financial planning, it's Suzy Orman.
- In cooking, it's Emeril LaGasse.
- In alternative health, it's Dr. Oz.
- In private space travel, it's Sir Richard Branson.
- In business growth, it's Charles Gaudet (okay, well … almost!).

Now, I'm not saying you have to be on television to become a trusted advisor, but the more you position yourself as a leading authority, the more in-demand you become and the bigger your profits.

---

[25] http://celebnetworth.org/kim-kardashian-net-worth-salary

As the leading authority, your payoffs include:

- increased fees,
- customers actively seeking you out,
- unequivocal credibility,
- partnership and endorsement opportunities, and
- thousands (possibly millions) of dollars in free media publicity.

It doesn't matter if you're a metal fabricator, corporate attorney, financial planner, executive coach, electrician, retailer, auto mechanic, or any other kind of business owner. Powerful examples can be found in every industry.

This chapter lays the groundwork for helping you become the "go-to" company in your industry—and that's more than being a "name." It's a positioning formula that involves niching, establishing trust, and knowing how to supply your name as the solution for your customers' needs.

~~~~

"This is the first time in history that word of mouth has become a digitally archived medium."

—Brett Hurt, founder and CEO, Bazaarvoice

~~~~

The Trust Factor

Positioning yourself as a trusted authority, a leading expert, and an industry celebrity is no longer an option. With my coaching clients, we've seen "big name" competitors with no marketing, no follow-up strategy, and less effective products outsell a superior product with better marketing by a 10-to-1 ratio. Why? Because when people repeatedly see and hear the name of a "famous" competitor related to *their* market, they assume your competitor is more knowledgeable, more credible, and more likely to deliver a better result. But being well-known isn't enough; people also have to trust you.

For various reasons, *trust* will be one of the biggest competitive advantages of this century. It's essential to your positioning as a leading authority.

~~~~

"We're about to see a merging of all the moments of truth. You'll be looking at a product on the shelf and using your cell phone to find information. You'll read reviews and then maybe you decide it's cool so you 'like' it for your friends, all within a minute.

"A consumer journey that once covered days, weeks or months just happened in a matter of seconds."

—Matt Moog, founder and CEO,
ViewPoints Network

~~~~

The value of gaining the trust of your clients or customers would be difficult to overestimate, especially considering how little trust consumers generally have. All too often, that's for good reason. Too many businesses make claims about the quality of their products or services, but they're unable to back them up.

One of the best resources for data on the public's trust of business and other institutions—such as governments and nonprofits—is the annual Edelman Trust Barometer. Edelman is, by its own account, the world's largest PR firm. For 12 years, the company has conducted surveys with 30,000 respondents in 25 countries to measure the trust attributed to public and private institutions.

~~~~

"Whether it's advertising via old standbys like TV, newspapers and radio or newer media like mobile and online, earning consumer trust is the holy grail of a successful campaign."

—Nielsen.com[26]

~~~~

---

[26] Nielsen. "Under the Influence: Consumer Trust in Advertising." September 17, 2013. http://www.nielsen.com/us/en/newswire/2013/under-the-influence-consumer-trust-in-advertising.html

Sadly, businesses don't fare well. According to the 2013 Edelman's Trust Barometer, only 18 percent of the general population trust business leaders to tell the truth regardless of how complex or unpopular that truth is.

According to Edleman's research, two of the largest concerns are:

- Placing profits ahead of customer interests, and
- Not having transparent and open business practices.

Let's face it, nobody wants to feel like the salesperson treats you nicely just to suck your wallet dry, right? Shrewd consumers know when companies place too much emphasis on making money and growing shareholder value. It almost always comes at the detriment of serving customers well and delivering the best value.

~~~~

"79 percent agree: 'Business is too concerned with profits and not enough with public responsibility.'"[27]

—The Futures Company

~~~~

Today, you can assume people in your market won't initially trust the quality of your service or your claims about your business in your advertising. Online consumer reviews are more powerful than any advertising message you could devise, no matter how catchy or sincere it is. Therefore, you simply can't rely on advertising alone.

~~~~

"People don't believe what you tell them.
They rarely believe what you show them.

---

[27] The Futures Company. "Risk and Responsibility: Marketing CSR in a Time of Economic Turmoil." September 20, 2011. [Available from: http://www.slideshare.net/futuresco/risk-and-responsibility]

They often believe what their friends tell them.
They always believe what they tell themselves."

—Seth Godin[28]

~~~~

Research proves people are more likely to trust a story told by a third party. Therefore, an advantage is attained through building publicity and broadcasting your trustworthy reputation.

~~~~

"When consumers hear about a product today, their first reaction is 'Let me search online for it.' And so they go on a journey of discovery: about a product, a service, an issue, an opportunity.

"Today you are not behind your competition. You are not behind the technology. You are behind your consumer."

—Riscad Tobaccowala, chief strategy
and innovation officer, VivaKi

~~~~

Be a Leader and Advisor

To differentiate yourself and establish your business as the clear choice for your target customers, assume the role of a leader. This requires taking the initiative to become a voice of authority for the community in your area of business. Create a virtuous cycle of positive publicity around you and your business by establishing connections with media representatives as well as respected local organizations and individuals—popular local bloggers, for example—who will boost your profile as an authority. Strive to leverage these trusted sources—media, nonprofit organizations, professional groups—to establish your credibility.

~~~~

[28] Seth Godin. "Belief". July 29, 2006.
http://sethgodin.typepad.com/seths_blog/2006/07/belief.html

*"You are not trying to sell **yourself** ever. Instead, customers try to sell themselves to you, convincing you to accept their money and help them. That result requires people being exposed to you. You have to have breadcrumbs all over the place, but they can't feel like they are being marketed to. As soon as they feel marketed to, they pull back."*

—Rich Schefren, Internet marketing strategist

~~~~

Which is more compelling: your ad in a newspaper—e.g., "I am the home interior painting expert"—or a news story in which the reporter describes you as "the home interior painting expert"? The second holds more credibility.

Because people generally trust the organizations they belong to, they tend to have faith in recommendations and endorsements coming from these groups. Engaging with group members socially and professionally can open the door to these. They can also lead to referrals beyond the group as members share information with their friends and professional peers.

Successful entrepreneurs typically use straightforward, no-cost, and easily deployed tactics to become the *trusted advisor* in their markets. But in my experience, many small business owners often fail to avail themselves of these tactics, perhaps believing they lack the knowledge to offer public advice or commentary.

Or you may be thinking, *Yeah right! Being an expert sounds great, but I'm no Donald Trump, Dr. Phil, or Martha Stewart.* Well, don't worry; you don't have to be. Consider again Ben McClure, co-owner of Gardner's Mattress & More. He has smartly used a set of tactics to position his relatively small store as the trusted sleep advisor. Specifically, Ben:

- Wrote a book about how to buy the right mattress, which he offers for free on his website,
- Created a sleep room where people can test a prospective mattress, and
- Focused his sales team on acting as sleep *advisors* rather than mattress salespeople.

McClure sums up what he and his company have been working to achieve this way:

> *"We like to think of ourselves as consumer advocates in the bedding industry. We're pulling back the covers—pardon the pun—on what everyone else in our industry is doing, without saying as much. Our customers seek us out because they've been frustrated with previous purchases, frustrated with a poor night's sleep, and frustrated by buying a mattress and not getting a better result."*

Had you ever heard of Ben McClure before? Probably not, unless quality sleep was important to you and you wanted to buy a mattress in Pennsylvania. Yet, he has achieved a powerful position within his market as a trusted authority and local industry celebrity. He's somebody like you—an entrepreneur doing his best to build his business.

Later this chapter highlights a series of methods for building your profile of trust through stories of successful business authorities. Each one features a single strategy or tactic; however, it's best to use more than one. Consider each of them and then create a portfolio of your own.

Get the Attention of the Media

Expert publicist Paul Hartunian knows how to leverage the media. We've spoken numerous times about the importance of publicity in establishing one's authority, summing up his beliefs this way:

> *"Whoever has the attention of the media wins. I don't care how small your business is and how large your competitors are. If you know how to get the attention of the media and they don't, you win."*

The media includes print, broadcast (TV and radio), and online. A weird phenomenon happens when people see you mentioned in the media. It instantly boosts your credibility, expert status, and (sometimes) offers fame. This is why I'm not at all bashful about mentioning the media channels I've been featured on, including Inc., Fox Business, and Forbes. I aim for positioning (and reinforcing that positioning) in my prospects' minds.

Getting mentioned in the media isn't as difficult as you might think. Imagine the challenge of coming up with a new story (sometimes several new stories) every single day of the year. The media hungers for good stories that will attract attention. They want experts who can offer advice and public commentary. Therefore, you want them to regard you as *the solution to their need for content*. You can be a big help by offering free content, which they'll absolutely appreciate.

In reaching out to media representatives, be aware of how best to approach each of them. The subtle but key differences are summarized here.

Use Press Releases for Print Coverage

The most effective method for garnering the attention of print media is issuing press releases regularly and consistently (ideally no less than twice a month). This results in being cited as an expert and earning coverage for your business that can lead to relationships with reporters and editors. It can afford you even more coverage, and before long, you become the go-to source for your specialized content.

You can use press releases to:

- Bring attention to yourself and your business when you receive an award,
- Release a new product or service,
- Develop an innovative solution to a common consumer problem,
- Announce an event you are holding,
- Spread the word about work you've done in the community,
- Recognize your customers or a specific customer for their loyalty or finding innovative uses for your product,
- Tell a specific story in which you're conveying your expertise, or
- Offer a controversial opinion on a popular topic.

Sending out press releases not only gets you coverage for a particular event, service announcement, or story; it will make the media aware of your availability as a source for a range of stories. The awareness generated can also lead to speaking engagements, additional media interviews, and other opportunities to share your opinions and expertise. The results might include:

- Increased trust and credibility,
- Growth in traffic to your website and/or retail stores,
- Higher search engine rankings, and
- More sales leads.

In fact, many Insiders' Club Members first discovered me by reading one of many articles featuring my advice, which drove them to my website. Often reporters reference points or information from my press releases to use in current articles, supplying me with free publicity.

Unlike advertising, a press release helps build trust because it's broadcast or published by a trusted third party. In fact, even if it's published exactly as you wrote it, it's most often perceived as if it came from the third party source originally.

Craft Effective Press Releases

Controversial stories or creating a unique perspective on a popular topic are key strategies for capturing attention, but they're not the only way. As Hartunian notes:

> *"Media people—and that includes newspaper reporters, talk show hosts, editors, producers, and many others—are always looking for a good story. You have plenty of good stories. I guarantee it. You just don't know how to spot them."*

Hartunian's examples display a diverse variety of entrepreneurs who could easily garner the attention of the media. They include:

- A landscaper who can talk about how to get rid of various rodents in gardens,

- A carpet cleaner who can tell reporters how to get stains out of carpets after Thanksgiving dinner,
- A dentist who can tell reporters whether those $20 teeth whitening kits from the drugstore are worth the money and effort, or
- A nutritionist who can tell reporters how to save money at the supermarket without compromising a family's health and nutrition.

It's best to be succinct in writing a headline and story, so it can be used by the newspaper with little editing. Communicate with the media in their preferred style and you'll greatly enhance the likelihood of getting your information picked up.

Remember to write your release from the perspective of a reporter rather than a business owner trying to sell something. Don't make the mistake of writing sales copy; save that for your advertising. Instead, provide useful information or highlight something your community will appreciate.

I recommend carefully reading articles in your local newspaper to get a feel for how reporters write. You'll notice a common framework your press release should replicate consisting of:

- A compelling headline.
- A succinct and compelling first paragraph of no more than two sentences (called a lede or lead in newspaper jargon) that pulls the reader into the story.
- A second paragraph that sums up the news value of the story (called the nut graph).
- A highly compelling quote from you that demonstrates your knowledge and expertise.
- A few paragraphs providing the specific information you want to share.
- Another compelling quote from you.
- A concluding statement.

Keep the length of the releases to about a page and make sure you provide your name, contact information, website URL, and a brief paragraph about you and your business. Press releases can be faxed, emailed, or even distributed online using a press release service. [29]

Meet the Needs of Broadcast Media

Broadcasters tend to respond to pitches via media release or by contacting them directly through email. Be sure to offer a strong idea for content to fill a segment of their show that will attract viewership. Again, focus on delivering a solution that bookers and producers need. Spend some time studying what makes it to air.

Remember, busy producers for local news and general interest shows are constantly on the hook for filling large amounts of broadcast time. They *need* content. The key is to develop your pitch in a way that meets the needs of their viewers, potentially goes against conventional wisdom (i.e., has a *man bites dog* quality to them), and is inexpensive to produce.

In your pitch, be sure to *show, not tell*. That is, show them the value of your information and expertise by giving them an example or story about something they probably know nothing about.

Once you've demonstrated you can deliver, broadcasters will continue to take interest in your ideas and reach out to you. Also, producers are professionally and personally connected to other producers—including people at their own station, the national network they're affiliated with, and other local and national networks. So, by building a strong relationship with a single local producer, you're opening the door to a web of connections.

"Stalk with Excellence"

For years, Jenn Lee, a noted life and small business coach in Central Florida, worked in real estate selling new homes and managing sales reps. While this work sustained her, Jenn never felt in control of her own career. As she notes:

---

[29] Example Press Releases and distribution resources can be found at http://www.PredictableProfitsPlaybook.com

"I woke up one day and realized I was tired of my bosses and coworkers always trying to 'filter' my enthusiasm for working, improving processes, and moving the ball forward. I always knew I had more to offer and was tired of being held back."

Recognizing she needed a change, Coach Jenn Lee (as she's now known) took her life in a new direction and, following her natural skills, founded her own coaching business. But how could she establish herself in a highly competitive consulting market? She described her solution this way: "I stalked with excellence."

First, she identified her target demographic—primarily women and solopreneurs—and then determined what they watch on TV and what magazines and newspapers they read.

"I wanted to pitch my local Fox TV affiliate that has my demographic in the morning hours. I thought about what's important to Fox and how they're trying to serve the public. Then I asked myself how I could provide a segment idea to help them do what they're trying to do and also get me what I need.

"To pitch them, I kept my message simple, consistent, and relevant so it served their audience. I initially pitched something about how to keep your New Year's Eve resolution and they took it. I also made it a bit contradictory by saying, 'Don't pick a New Year's Eve resolution.'

"Since delivering on that pitch, I've worked at maintaining a good relationship with key people at Fox, which isn't hard because I like them. I get called all the time to help them out, which helps me out."

Coach Jenn Lee has positioned herself as a go-to source not only for Fox but for a range of other print and broadcast media. She has also leveraged her expertise to garner speaking engagements at forums, seminars, trade shows, and professional groups. As a result, she's received tens of thousands, possibly millions, of dollars' worth of publicity for free.

Today, she has a thriving coaching practice and an audience of thousands whom she serves weekly through her blog and *Mogovation Newsletter*. She reaches thousands more through her speaking engagements across the country.

Why Speaking Is Important

Take a moment to think of the three most influential people of the last 50 years—dead or alive. While a significant amount of variation will exist between them, I can all but guarantee all three have two qualities in common: (1) They are or were public speakers, and (2) they've published a book or other critical form of written content such as newspaper columns, essays, or reports. Whether it's Sir Richard Branson, Tony Robbins, Bill Gates, Jeff Bezos, Tony Hsieh or the late Steve Jobs, public speaking has played a critical role in establishing their influence.

Those are mighty big shoes to fill, but as with all the entrepreneurs cited in this book, their efforts started within their defined markets, and their reputations grew from there. You can do the same.

For example, when Siamak Taghaddos and David Houser, the founders of telecommunications provider Grasshopper, first went into business, all they knew was they wanted to serve entrepreneurs. After their research showed unmet telecommunications needs existed among entrepreneurs, they were off and running with Grasshopper. To promote it, they began giving speeches. As Taghaddos recalls:

> *"David and I got involved in the entrepreneur community by speaking at relevant and respected events whenever and wherever we could. The goal was to make Grasshopper synonymous with being in entrepreneurship as well as being run by entrepreneurs—knowledgeable, successful ones people looked up to.*
>
> *"This gave them a sense that we know what we're talking about. Word-of-mouth conversion for us has gone through the roof. Now, more than half of our business comes through referrals."*

They built their credibility by demonstrating their expertise, articulating their market's problems, and offering strong solutions. They also gained credibility through the implicit endorsement of the organizations that hosted their speeches.

Paul Lemberg, who started his consulting business from humble circumstances, conveys this story:

"When I first started business coaching back in 1995, there weren't any models for how to do this. I just started doing it with no idea how to market it.

"However, I quickly figured out that if I speak to people, I could get them interested—but I had never spoken before. I put together a program that in 1995 was somewhat revolutionary and probably wasn't particularly good—but it rocked people.

"I found that no matter where I spoke, I got a reaction. I once spoke at a Kiwanis Club. It was dark and lunch had been served. One old guy snored in the middle of it. Then as I was walking out the door, the president of the organization came up to me and said, 'That was an amazing presentation. I've never seen them so animated!'

"I thanked him, but I still just wanted to get out the door when a woman grabbed my arm. She told me what I said was amazing, asked how much I charge, and hired me.

"Every time I spoke—and I tell you I was terrible—people would still hear my message."

Lemberg continued to share his insights on business, speaking at any organization that would have him. It won him a lot of business. To date, he has helped his clients generate more than $350 million in profits and has grown his business into a highly sought-after and profitable service. In fact, his clients include Cisco, Goldman Sachs, Adobe, ADI, and many other notable companies.

Become a Columnist, Blogger, or Author

You could also pitch the idea of delivering a regular column for a newspaper or website, or even create your own blog. Ben McClure recounts:

"One thing we've done that has worked incredibly well to establish trust is to write a column called 'Slumber' in a prominent, high-end publication called Finer Living Lancaster. *This column gives us an opportunity to tell a bit more of our story. I can use humor or real-life stories to relay the message to our readers. Customers tell me they're*

shopping at Gardner's because they appreciate reading about my own bed or my candid thoughts about sleep and why they should consider investing in a better night's sleep."

Internet marketing strategist and business growth expert Rich Schefren provides a powerful example with his Internet Business Manifesto. He and his company, Strategic Profits, have earned such a strong reputation that clients *sell themselves to him.*

However, it didn't always work this way. As he tells it:

> *"I was a business coach and my clients tended to get phenomenal results, some becoming very well known on the Internet. But it bothered me that I didn't have more clients, though I didn't have any products and I didn't do much marketing either.*
>
> *"Back then, I was a behind-the-scenes guy who people went to due to word of mouth. When I was coaching, I'd usually coach a group of people at a time. Usually these engagements lasted for a year and a half.*
>
> *"One group that represented sixty percent of my income was coming to an end. Another would start in three months. But I was concerned. I wanted to pick up some coaching clients for about three months. This is when I wrote my report* Internet Business Manifesto *and put it on my blog.*
>
> *"I was hoping to get it out there and pick up maybe twenty clients. However, lo and behold, it went viral. About thirty-five thousand people opted in and downloaded it in the first couple of weeks, and more than two thousand people wanted to become my clients. As soon as I opened up taking clients, more than a million dollars was sent to my PayPal account. I did about three and a half million in that first four or five weeks. Since then, the* Manifesto *has been downloaded one-and-a-half million times and been responsible for a little over ten million in sales.*
>
> *"That little thirty-page report took me from someone completely unknown in the industry to one of the most well-known coaches with tremendous amounts of power and recognition. I went from worrying about where to get my next client to consistently raising my prices because I don't want more clients. My business does, but not me.*

"With my reports and marketing, over time I've left trails of breadcrumbs all over the Internet for people to read about my accomplishments and what my company does. A good portion of them will ultimately become clients."

Great Content Distributed Through Social Media

Another entrepreneur, Sarah Robinson, was running a modest practice as a small business consultant when she changed her focus to mompreneurs.

To attract their attention, she started a blog called *The Maverick Mom*. Before long, though, she concluded that to achieve her professional and financial goals, she'd have to broaden her focus. She had also noticed those reading her blog weren't exclusively mompreneurs. So she did two things a blogger should never do: She changed the name of her blog to *Escaping Mediocrity* and changed the blog's URL. This meant she had to continue to build her following *and* transition the community she had built over three months to a new URL with a new blog name. No easy task.

To build momentum for the new blog, for her, it came down to producing strong content and being active in social media channels. As she says:

> *"I wrote about things that everybody else was too scared to write about—what it was truly like to be an entrepreneur—and one of my most popular posts was called Failing Sucks. I was tired of people talking about how great it is to fail. It annoyed me that we were supposed to skim over how crappy it feels to fail and move straight into this grand learning experience, which failing absolutely is. But to skip over that 'it feels really crappy' part when you're in the middle of it is a mistake.*
>
> *"So I positioned all of my content around 'this is what it really feels like,' not the glossy polished-for-the-camera experience. Today, a ton of people are doing that, but at the time, there weren't. People really gravitated toward that message.*
>
> *"It was about putting out honest and strong content in a counterintuitive way. And you should see the emails I got. Friends wrote, 'I can't believe you just wrote about that.' Well, I'm not going to lie. My whole brand of*

Escaping Mediocrity *is built on telling people what the experience is. Saying 'You get through it' made people feel normal.*

"People in the comments section of the blog started to build this incredible community of support, so the blog functioned whether I was present or not."

Sarah shares how she attracted people to her blog:

"I talked to people through social media because I'm not one to only post outgoing messages. Doing only that is a dumb use of social media. After all, it's called SOCIAL media.

"So I'd have conversations with people and put out memes—mostly questions that reflect the brand of the blog, such as 'What can you do to help a client today to provoke conversations via Twitter, my natural habitat, and on Facebook and other sources?' And I would tag them with Escaping Mediocrity. *People would respond and we'd have conversations, and that would lead people to my blog. I also had a newsletter that went out, and this helped create more word of mouth.*

"I might add that my community of supporters at Escaping Mediocrity *were my biggest brand advocates, championing my blog on days when I was lagging. They'd pick up the banner and lead the charge."*

Within a few months, Robinson had built a subscriber base of about 5,000 for her blog and newsletter. Before long, she had a consistent community of 20,000 people following and engaging with the blog. In all, these efforts helped her create an incredibly powerful word-of-mouth engine. A leading editor and publisher found her, which led to her book *Fierce Loyalty: Unlocking the DNA of Wildly Successful Communities.* She has turned the name of the book into a new consulting business, which has further increased her reputation and cash flow.

Write a Book

As touched on earlier, another smart tactic is to write a book. Ben McClure did so, and he offers it for free at his store and on his website. At 28 pages, it's no doorstopper. But it offers good advice about how to make the best mattress purchase possible.

You don't have to be an accomplished author—you can even hire a freelance writer to help you. Your goal is to create a succinct book or informative report that educates those in your target market on your product or service. As McClure notes:

> *"Nobody else in our industry wrote a book about how to buy a bed. Basically, it identifies the mistakes made when mattress shopping and how to avoid those mistakes. Although this seems like a relatively simple thing to do, our customers find it extremely helpful, and it further establishes us as their sleep advisor."*

On one of our regular Insiders' Club conference calls, I illustrated the importance of writing a book using the example of a financial planner. Picture this: Say you were looking to hire a financial planner to help you structure your retirement. You narrowed your choices down to two contacts—both people offering similar benefits—but one of them said, "While my competitor offers valid points, I would like to present you with my book for a more in-depth look at your situation because *I wrote the book* on how to retire wealthy." Voila. The author becomes an instant source of credibility.

Think about all the well-known names I've mentioned: Martha Stewart, Donald Trump, Sir Richard Branson, Dr. Phil, Dr. Oz, Tony Robbins, and so forth. What do they all have in common? *They have at least one book!*

Is the purpose of their book to get rich as an author? Absolutely not. It's to establish credibility and expert status—the *only* reason to write a book. And with the advancements in technology today, anyone can write a book, self-publish it, and distribute it through various online channels such as Amazon.com.

Follow Two Principles with All Communications

1. Stand Out and Dare to Be Different

It's important to leverage what's unique about you and your business. All press releases and media pitches need to focus on what you uniquely have to offer viewers, listeners, or readers. The media representatives want to know how you can help their audiences and thereby better serve their markets. But be sure to avoid *telling* them you are a unique expert; *show* them by providing unique, important information.

Siamak Taghaddos shares his thoughts:

> *"Companies don't stand out when they try to do what they have heard or copy others. For example, to be the expert in your industry, all the books say give a lot of seminars, write a lot of content, and tell everyone you're an expert. That sounds good in theory, but it says nothing about how it should be executed in a way that's unique to the business.*
>
> *"It's about finding what makes you unique—and you don't have to try too hard because it comes naturally. For example, what if you're a guy who owns a paint store and you want to establish an amazing local presence in the community. Conventional wisdom would tell you to put on a show or event, and then take out an ad with a cheesy jingle and so on.*
>
> *"But what if you paint the home of a single mother struggling to raise her children? You do this well and news spreads by word of mouth and through the media that you're helpful in the community? If you, as the paint store owner, have been in the community for a long time and you care about people, then that's authentic and unique. And that's how you establish yourself without spending much money."*

Simply stated, advertising is when, in one form or another, you tell the client you are different. Positioning is when you clearly show the client *how and why* you are different.

2. Focus on Leaving the Recipient Better Off Having Seen Your Material

One of my early mentors told me: "If you can define your prospects' problems better than they can, they will automatically assume you have the solution to their problem." So my coaching clients must be able to understand and fully articulate their clients' problems before offering the solution. And explain those problems better than their clients do.

For example, after working awhile with a new client to help him grow his business, I pointed out that, when he hired me, he never asked about me in detail. I had focused our initial conversation on his goals, what his challenges were, and which opportunities he wanted to maximize. He responded that he felt I fully understood him and what he was experiencing better than anyone else he had talked with. In this way, I was able to display an intimate knowledge of his pain clearly and concisely, followed with a solution. As soon as he made this realization, he assumed I had the information, tools, and expertise to guide him. I've since helped him grow his small business by over $7,500,000—and I still haven't had to sell him on how smart I am.

Paul Lemberg shares a similar experience this way:

"I learned—and this is not revolutionary—that I can build trust by doing something trustworthy, which was to keep putting out super-high-quality information. I share as much as I can."

Clearly, if you help people solve their problems and share authentic stories that *show* your expertise rather than *tell* them about it, word will spread fast and your business will boom.

SECTION III:
PRODUCT/SERVICE DOMINATION

Chapter 5:
Escaping the Commodity Trap

"People can have the Model T in any color—so long as it's black."
—Henry Ford, founder, Ford Motor Co.

MANY ONCE-MIGHTY companies have suffered terribly due to a failure to innovate and meet, if not exceed, the demands of the *New Consumer*. These companies include Blockbuster, Eastman Kodak, Blackberry, Compaq, and Borders Books and Music.

To keep your business moving forward and eventually dominating your market requires the continual creation of greater value and advantage for your clients. That means evolving your offerings to meet changing consumer needs and desires. By doing this, you avoid becoming a commodity as tastes and needs change. In effect, you own a powerful solution to the consumer's immediate need or desire.

~~~~

"Contrary to popular practice, companies that achieve breakout performance employ structured methods to link future and emerging consumer needs with long-term investment decisions."[30]

—Marketing Leadership Council

~~~~

---

[30] *Report by the Marketing Leadership Council,* 2008.

Provide Unique Value

This chapter addresses how your product or service helps convince the *New Consumer* that you are the obvious choice. You do this by avoiding the *commodity trap*. That's when consumers view your product or service as one among many rather than a unique solution with high value. In fact, as an entrepreneur or small business owner, you risk allowing your product or service to exist as a commodity.

As Marshall Thurber once told me, "All the king's men and horses are helpless in the face of a product that has more value."[31] Perhaps the most notable example of this point is billionaire entrepreneur Sir Richard Branson. He founded every one of his companies on delivering the most value possible to his target market of consumers—even if that value was simply offering a better customer experience. The goal? *To far exceed what anyone else in that market was currently delivering.*

This may seem obvious, but it's important to state because this philosophy helped make Branson (and many others) a lot of money. As *Strategic Entrepreneurs,* we know that when we deliver the most value and benefit to the *New Consumer*, we will be paid in proportion to that value. In other words, value drives profits.

~~~~

"Commoditization—what I see as the cancer of the 21st century commerce— has fueled ferocious price competition, leading to lower prices, margins and profits for businesses. With price as the only real differentiator, producers are left with a challenge: They must find a way to stand out in the crowd."[32]

—Peter Georgescu, chairman emeritus and
former CEO, Young & Rubicam

~~~~

Anyone can sell a can of paint. But consider the additional appeal of a home improvement solution that increases the value of your most valuable

---

[31] A quote borrowed from Walter Bigelow Wriston (August 3, 1919–January 19, 2005). He was former chairman and CEO of CitiCorp.

[32] Nulman, A. *Pow! Right Between the Eyes: Profiting from the Power of Surprise.* 2009: Wiley. p. 272.

asset. Anyone can sell shoes, but only Zappos and Toms[33] sell a solution to the experience of buying shoes. One provides service so exceptional that the shopping experience is transformed, and the other makes purchasing a pair of shoes an altruistic act.

In either case, if you were to strip away the added value—home improvement or shoe-buying extras—then you'd be left with a can of paint or a pair of shoes. Both are commodities, so you would then need to compete on price.

Today, escaping the commodity trap requires making choices about your product or service that enhance its perceived value and overall benefit. Such added value answers these key questions asked by the *New Consumer*:

- Will this purchase help me look good to my family, friends, and professional peers?
- Will I be able to justify this purchase to my spouse, friends, family, and professional peers and sound like a smart buyer?
- Can I be sure I'm not wasting my money?
- Will I get the result I'm after?
- Will the company stand behind my purchase?
- Will it be easy and stress-free to work with this company?
- Will this purchase make me feel good because I'm doing good? (Like helping a charity by purchasing from Toms, for example, or buying "green" products or services.)

~~~~

"The status bubble: Consumers aren't interested in you per se; they're interested in what an association with you means for them. Without total information on you, they risk compromising their ethics, sustainability and social responsibility."[34]

—TrendWatching.com

~~~~

---

[33] See Chapter 3.
[34] TrendWatching.com. *The Trend Report.* 2013.

For example, Walter Bergeron, founder of Power Control Services[35], competes in a highly commoditized industry. His company provides repair services for circuit boards used by large industrial manufacturers. While these repairs require a certain degree of skill and experience, they're not so difficult that the technical challenge presents a barrier to entry in his market. Therefore, many of his competitors compete on price and turnaround time.

Although Bergeron's company provides quality and has a highly competitive turnaround time, these weren't enough to dominate his industry, so he has added this compelling *value proposition* to his set of services:

> *"Our [value proposition] used to be around the motto: Five-day repair the right way right away. However, this has become commoditized as the rest of the industry has realized what we're doing and has copied it. It's no longer enough to avoid being a commodity.*
>
> *"So we looked at what we do and who we serve, their needs and concerns, and concluded they would favorably respond to having their equipment repaired once and then never paying for it again. When we say this, it intrigues them. They ask how that can be when everyone else provides a warranty for only one or two years on that equipment. Well, we are granting a lifetime warranty on each piece of equipment we repair for a customer. We'll repair any piece of equipment we've serviced every single time it fails in the future for free. We'll even pay for shipping, and we'll do it as a rush.*
>
> *"This came about as we sought to bundle our services into a higher value package. We call it our Platinum Rebuild Program, which has helped us escape being viewed as a commoditized service because everyone else is offering a standard repair program."*

I love Bergeron's story; it captures nearly everything needed to escape the commodity trap. Bergeron researched his customers' pain, developed a value proposition to address their needs, and clearly answered the questions of the *New Consumer* affirmatively. As a result, he's offering the Platinum

---

[35] Walter Bergeron's company was sold in December 2012, right after this interview was conducted. This was due to his extraordinary ability to grow his company. The sale price was significant enough that Walter says, "I can finally live a lifetime like few people can …"

package at a slightly higher price point than other programs. In effect, he's created mutual value for his customers and his company.

Do you remember what Amazon did in its early years? Rather than peel more money from customers through higher prices, this online retailer looked for ways to deliver increased value. After its leaders learned their customers wanted a more satisfying purchase experience, the site provided product reviews and a simplified buying process. These features became incredibly popular and helped turn Amazon into a multibillion-dollar company.

Delivering Value is a Mindset

Creating a compelling *value proposition* requires a deep understanding of your market's needs and desires. This isn't possible without the right mindset. It's more than simply making money. Rather, it's to make irresistible offers that support people and, if possible, carry a high social or moral purpose.

In fact, without the right mindset, you risk misidentifying the true needs and desires of your market, you could fall flat in your efforts or, worse, be perceived as cheap and inauthentic.

~~~~

"A recent survey of 9,000 decision makers in B2B companies found that 86% of the 'unique benefits' touted by vendors were not perceived as unique or having enough impact to create preference."[36]

—Tim Reister, Chief Strategy and Marketing Officer
of Corporate Visions Inc.

~~~~

Unwittingly, it appears, companies are creating value-parity positions, not value propositions, which will soon be discussed. First, however, let's address the challenges posed by marginal entrepreneurs and what the *New Consumer* expects.

---

[36] Riester, T. "Three B2B Value-Proposition Rules That Create Preference, Not Just Parity." 2010. [Available from: http://www.marketingprofs.com/articles/2010/3491/three-b2b-value-proposition-rules-that-create-preference-not-just-parity]

What the Strategic Entrepreneur is Up Against

I spoke with Kevin Hallenbeck, a principal at Sandler Training[37] and one of the most professional and talented consultative sales coaches I've ever met. As such, he takes a dim view of salespeople who fail to understand the true purpose of business:

> *"One of my classic lines is that selling ice to Eskimos is unethical. If people think a great sales person is someone who can sell somebody something they don't need or want, I heartily disagree. These are salespeople who do nothing more than try to sell what they have in inventory, whether you need it or not. If they need to unload minivans when you come in for a sports car, they'll do their best to convince you that you need a minivan.*
>
> *"For some reason, we celebrate the salesperson who does this. However, I would argue that this type of salesperson is dying, obsolete. A certain number of salespeople will always be that way, but they're hacks and con artists who base their selling on trickery and manipulation. That's flat out not the way to develop an enduring business. It's the way to sell something and then get out of town and run."*

The Growth Factor Question

Hallenbeck's mindset of helping people get what they want and need is an essential one to adopt when growing your business. You can do this by constantly asking what I've termed *The Growth Factor* question: "What else can I do for my clients or customers that will give them a greater value, benefit and experience to help them achieve the ultimate result they are after?"

However, growing your business doesn't necessarily involve adding new products or services continually (although it can be important).

---

[37] Sandler Training helps companies and sales professionals increase their sales effectiveness through training, coaching, and consulting. Using a nontraditional consultative selling approach, Sandler crafts solutions that go beyond simply training salespeople and sales managers.

Growing your business derives from *creating greater value and advantage and then articulating these to the client or customer.*

When you look for an accountant, for example, you're not just looking for a number cruncher. You're looking for someone who will give you peace of mind that you're maximizing tax deductions while remaining compliant with tax laws. When you go to a barber or hair salon, you're not simply looking for a haircut. Rather, you want to feel confident about how you look as well as have a relaxing and pleasant experience.

Benefits Over Features

Jay Abraham, one of the most successful business and marketing strategists of our time, argues that the features of any product or service have little marketing significance unless you can demonstrate their benefit or value to the customer. It's not about the can of paint, but what the paint allows the customer to do, as noted in his book:

> *"With regard to influence and persuasion, keep in mind the key is benefits over features. Features are only useful if you can show their benefits.*
>
> *"If I were selling you televisions or electronic equipment, I might tell you a particular model has a twenty-feature split-screen capacity to boggle your mind. That's a feature. If I were to describe the benefit of this feature, I might say something like this: 'Marty, how'd you like to be able to watch all seven stations concurrently and, if you especially like what's happening on one station, be able to preserve what's happening on the others and come back and watch them later? Well, this multi-circuit storage memory, twelve-function system gives you that capability.'*
>
> *"Remember ... most people are obsessed with selling features, but features are meaningless in and of themselves. The benefits of the features are what life is all about, what selling is all about, and what marketing is all about.*
>
> *"If you want preeminence, dominance, and success on a perpetual basis, benefits are where you'll focus your understanding and attention. Ask: What is the spectrum of benefits or results my product, service, or company produce*

and render? What are they short term and long term, tangibly and intangibly, measurably and emotionally for the customer?"[38]

~~~~

"A recent study by the Weatherhead School of Management at Case Western Reserve University confirmed what we already know in our heart of hearts—satisfaction has little to do with loyalty. What was a surprise to them, however, was clear evidence that trust wasn't the deciding factor, either—at least not trust alone. What customers are looking for first and foremost is value—not the monetary kind of value, but value that impacts a person's life.

"To determine the real, loyalty-building value of your products and services, you have to go beyond the features, functions and processes we are all so fond of and look instead at two critical factors: the value your offering brings to a customer's life and how the experiences that surround and support your offering add to or detract from that value."[39]

—Diane LaSalle

~~~~

Mike Michalowicz expresses this another way through his 95/5 Rule. (Earlier, Michalowicz noted how he used the concepts outlined here to add rocket fuel to his computer network integration company.) He says entrepreneurs and small business people need to focus on the five percent of their product or service that leads to 95 percent of the conversations with customers and clients. He describes his 95/5 Rule this way:

"We had a suite of services we offered, and everything we did was integrated into that suite. However, we led with six distinguishing things and, while that was five percent of the work we would do, it was ninety-five percent of the conversation and ninety-five percent of the customer's interest.

"When you go to a dentist he doesn't give you all the details of everything he does in a normal exam. What you really care about are the things he does infrequently, such as fix your tooth when you have pain. You'll gladly pay a

---

[38] Abraham, J. *How to Think Like a Marketing Genius.* 2005: The Abraham Group, Inc.
[39] LaSalle, D. "Experiencing Value." 2003. [cited 2012; Available from: http://www.marketingprofs.com/3/lasalle1.asp]

premium to alleviate that pain, even though it only represents about five per-cent of the work the dentist delivers.

"We have to be deliberate about the five percent distinctions and put our emphasis on developing them, keeping them updated and fresh, and communi-cating them to the market."

Your Value Proposition

The Growth Factor question is all about finding, adding, and optimizing value-adds of your product or service that strike directly at the basis of the *New Consumer's* buying decision. That means rather than focusing on new prod-ucts or services for business growth, you emphasize your *value proposition.* The right one is like honey to the *New Consumer.*

However, it's easy to misidentify what consumers truly want. What can you do to avoid that mistake and develop an effective *value proposition?*

Be a Consultant, Not a Salesperson

As an old saying goes, when someone walks into a hardware store looking for a drill, they actually wants holes. And as a strategic entrepreneur, you must know the real need for the tool in order to provide the best result possible. For example, a seasoned construction worker dealing with metal framework has much different needs than the do-it-yourself homeowner installing shelves. So to serve them, you'd act as a consultant and add value to the purchase of a drill from you. Being a consultant rather than a sales-man involves being fully customer-centric in your thinking. That means you place a high priority on exceeding the customer's expectations as you solve his problems.

If you sell paint, your customers may define value in terms of how easy you make it for them to beautifully paint their houses, attract buyers, or make them look good in the eyes of their neighbors. Kevin Hallenbeck describes the basis of consultative selling this way:

"We're talking about someone who has a deep knowledge and under-standing of the marketplace they're selling into. They ask questions to find out individual prospects' needs; the problems they face; the challenges they

*have. They engage in a dialogue, a conversation. It's not a one-way experience
in which the salesperson talks and the prospect listens to the pontificating."*

By anticipating the wants and needs of your customers, you'll bring them closer to you. After all, most people feel underappreciated in their work and at home, and they often crave feeling valued, special, and appreciated. Zappos does this well in many ways. The company offers reviews in which others can learn of the strengths and weaknesses of particular products. Its customer service people are well trained to understand the customers' needs and even create demonstration videos displaying product attributes. Thus, Zappos acts as a consultant to help customers choose the best product for their needs. Then the company takes it a step further to truly "wow" anyone who contacts Zappos with extraordinary customer service.

~~~~

*"Whatever you do, do it well. Do it so well that when people see you do it,
they will want to come back and see you do it again and they will want to
bring others and show them how well you do what you do."*

—Walt Disney

~~~~

Don't Assume You Are Your Market

It's not uncommon for me to hear my coaching clients say *I am my market.* That is, they used to be the exact person they're marketing to today. Or they say they have a shared experience with the people in their market that connects them to the needs and desires of those they want to serve.

However, *you* are not your market. Continuing to believe that will only cause you to misidentify the needs and desires of your customers. It's a simple fact that, by becoming an entrepreneur or small business owner, you have evolved away from the people you want to serve. You are *no longer* a plumber, an investor, a human resources manager or whatever you came from.

Instead, you are in the business of marketing ways to solve their problems and create value *as your prospect defines it.* You may be uniquely positioned to speak with individuals in your market, but you're removed from their needs and desires and unable to clearly define what they are today or in the future. And I'm not the only one saying this; Hallenbeck and many others with expertise in this area concur.

In fact, when I spoke with Anne Holland, principal of Anne Holland Ventures, Inc., she readily agreed. Holland is a journalist and publisher of WhichTestWon.com, the world's largest case study library of A/B marketing tests. She's become an expert on helping entrepreneurs avoid common missteps and sharpen their messaging. She emphasizes that entrepreneurs make a big mistake if they assume they themselves are their market:

> *"No matter how close you think you are, you are not your market. No matter how smart you are, how much market research you've done, how much you understand your marketplace, how many years of marketing experience you have, and how well you know all the best practices, you will never be sure ... You're only guessing.*
>
> *"Testing shows all of this. It shows that even people who are unbelievable experts don't get it right every time. It's because you aren't the person you are selling to. You can't help that; you're the marketer or the person who owns the company, or you're the person who knows a lot about your product and why it's so great. But you are not the prospect. Only the prospect can tell you if you have the best offer."*

Value Is Driven By the Customer or Client

When you *truly listen* to your customer or client, you may be surprised by what you hear. For this reason, allow the benefits you add to your product or service to be driven by the people you serve.

~~~~

> *"Before doing anything, your prospects want to easily determine whether you can solve their problem in a way that makes sense to them. To do that, you have to do the following:*

- *Use language they use. Don't force them to learn new buzzwords or acronyms, and don't assume they are as familiar with analysts' terms as you are.*
- *Keep it simple. You get only a slice of their time and attention. Don't waste it.*
- *Convey clearly and specifically how you will help them.*
- *Indicate who you solve problems for."*[40]

—Kathryn Roy

~~~~

I've seen this approach in my own consulting. I worked with an incredibly talented trading educator with a host of valuable products and services to help traders get better at what they do.

When we started working together, it would have been easy for us to believe the people seeking financial education and related products and services merely wanted to be rich. This assumption was reinforced when we looked at how almost all of his competitors marketed themselves. However, we knew better and did our homework.

We discovered that people in his market wanted more than to make money. Specifically, they wanted to supplement their income, come closer to becoming full-time traders, spend more time with their families, and be proud of what they're doing with their lives. They wanted a higher quality of life without the stress of working more hours.

These insights didn't come from the inside out; they were driven by information we collected from his clients. In effect, the clients drove the value.

Walter Bergeron has also learned this lesson well. Remember his company's Platinum Rebuild Program featuring a lifetime warranty on each piece of equipment the company fixes? This has been an incredibly valuable service offering for them, and customer input drove his decision to offer it. As Bergeron explains:

---

[40] Roy, K. "Don't Make These Value Proposition Mistakes." 2009. [Available from: http://www.marketingprofs.com/articles/2009/3212/dont-make-these-value-proposition-mistakes]

"The value is driven by the customer and not by what you have to offer. Once you find out what their need is—that's the real trick, and it may change—fill it the best you can.

"Our original idea was to put together the Platinum Rebuild Program with a two-year warranty, which was double what everybody else in our industry was offering. We thought that would be great. However, we went to our customers and asked what their true needs were. One of the things they said is, 'We don't want to have to worry about the equipment once you repair it. And we don't want to have to pay for it again in the five- or ten-year life of each piece of equipment.'

"So that told us the value is in never having to worry about it again, not only for one or two or three years but ever. Doing this eliminated the risk of any of our competitors increasing their warranty by one or two or three years. In addition, we eliminated the entire objection of our customers and gave them more value based on what their actual needs were, not what we wanted to provide."

Always Talk to Clients

Greg Habstritt is the founder of Simple Wealth, a business growth consultancy, and president of the Real Equity Group of Companies, a private investment firm he founded in 2001. In addition to these companies, Habstritt has founded, built, and sold more than 20 companies. He has received numerous citations and awards for his entrepreneurial spirit and business success.

With his track record, you might think Habstritt would intuitively understand the needs and desires of the people in the markets he serves. And yet, he's continually surprised by what he finds when he talks to clients. As he says:

"Most entrepreneurs tell themselves they know their market really well, but they're wrong because they've never come out and asked the question. As an example, one of my businesses is Vets to Go, which is a veterinary house-call service, and I have a partner who's a veterinarian. When we first started down this path, I asked her, 'Why do people hire you? And why do they call you to their house?' She answered just as I did and just as others I spoke to

did, which was, 'I'm a busy person and visiting the veterinarian with a couple of dogs is really inconvenient.'

"However, think about this from the perspective of people who care about their dogs, which is our target market. So I said to her, 'I get that convenience is a big driver, but have you ever asked your clients why they chose you?' She said she never had, so for the next 30 days, she asked every client she saw the single biggest reason they had her come to their home.

"She was blown away by their answers. She told me, 'I would have bet my life it was about the convenience and less hassle and time. Surprisingly, ninety-seven percent of the clients said it was because it put less stress on their pet. That was the driving force for them to hire her.

"So the entire marketing orientation of our business changed overnight when we came up with the tagline 'Stress-free pet care in the comfort of your own home.'"

Do you see how everything you do to create your *value proposition* needs to connect with the people in your market?

Stay Ahead of the Curve

The business world constantly changes. All entrepreneurs or small business people who believe they have customers lapping at their hand are marginal entrepreneurs and doomed to fail.[41] Market forces and the evolving nature of the *New Consumer* mean that what's true today may be untrue in a year.

~~~~

"Today's best brands are in touch with their own humanity and the humanity of others. They listen to consumers, employees, and investors alike and respond to the messages they receive. They want to know how people really feel about their company, they gather input and use it to drive innovation, and they realize that there is a lot to be learned from the wisdom of crowds. The

---

[41] Consider the once mighty Microsoft. It's been a monolith in the computing world, but the biggest threat it faces is a failure to adapt as quickly as competitors to changes in technology. For example, Office is challenged by Google Docs and other cloud-based software, and Windows Surface has not won the hearts of iPad users.

challenge for brands is to respond quickly and with sincerity, or they risk compromising the relationship.

"After all, brands evoke emotion. They are personal. They fulfill and delight us. They are reliable, familiar, exciting, surprising, and ever in the backdrop of our lives. They are woven into our memories, fantasies, and dreams. They have the power to touch and change us precisely because they are human creations, invented in response to both our deepest and most practical needs and desires."[42]

—Jez Frampton, Global Chief Executive, Interbrand

~~~~

Regarding the need for adaptability, my friend Marshall Thurber coined the term *DyVal* by combining the words *dynamic* and *value*. As Thurber explains:

"This idea of DyVal is a critical concept for business today, based on the metaphor that you're constantly surfing on liquid turf. If you're going to succeed, you have to be out there adapting your DyVal based on what's happening because you need to see the next wave before it hits. The surfer who's not awake gets busted and crashes, and that's basically what happens in business."

The Right Market Theory

Thurber adds that anticipating the next wave requires being aware of the forces influencing your market as well as how your offering reflects these changes. This involves having the right *market theory*, which allows you to anticipate change and correctly adapt to it. Thurber continues:

"The question to ask is what's changing in the dynamic? Then adjust before it does. If you wait until it's already happening, you're behind the curve. So questions last far longer than answers.

---

[42] Jez Frampton, C.G.O.I. "The Future is Human." 2012. [cited 2012; Available from: http://www.interbrand.com/en/best-global-brands/2012/the-human-issue.aspx]

"Once you're anticipating changes, you don't have to be right that many times, but when you are, that advantage can sustain the 'life is good' phase.

"The ultimate acid test of a theory is predictability. You see, all of the king's men and horses are helpless in the face of a product that has more value than the offer it's replacing. So a good DyVal is predictable as well as dynamic. And it adds value in a way that supports people while having a high social or moral purpose. When you've found that, go there because that's sustainable."

Bergeron's company with its lifetime warranty provides a good case in point. He operates in a highly dynamic market in which competitors were closing in guarantees—a key differentiator for his company. He was pro-actively asking the right questions, and he was able to make well-targeted adjustments based on a desire to deliver even greater value—*DyVal*—to his clients. This, in turn, led to significant market and financial gains for his company.

Now, once you've been able to discern exactly what your clients or customers most want and you've built that value into your product or service, what will you do with your prices? The next chapter addresses that question.

Chapter 6:
How to Raise Your Prices

"Price is what you pay. Value is what you get."
—Warren Buffet, business magnate,
investor, and philanthropist

WHEN TALKING ABOUT price, I think of terms such as *elasticity, price point,*[43] *value perception, The Growth Factor,*[44] and *price as differentiator.*

Notice I didn't include such terms as *discount, price cuts,* and *low price position.*[45]

Too many entrepreneurs have responded to the challenges of recent years by engaging in fierce price wars. But that's a race to the bottom. All too often, the demands of cheap prices lead to:

- Inadequate customer service,
- Cheapened products and services,
- More costly penny-pinching customers and clients,
- Tight-to-nonexistent profit margins,

---

[43] See Chapter 2 to learn more about *price point.*
[44] See Chapter 5 for a full discussion of *The Growth Factor.*
[45] You can distinguish yourself—or more likely *extinguish* yourself—by offering the lowest price in the market.

- Inability to grow margins, and
- A devalued perception among consumers concerning the quality of your products and services as well as your business.

In the end, even if you win a price war—a highly dubious claim because someone will always offer a cheaper price—you will still lose.

If, instead, you continually focus on delivering better value, you'll be able to increase your prices even while increasing demand for your products and services. You can, in fact, leverage a higher *price point* to communicate greater quality and value to prospective clients or customers.

Because *New Consumers* are most often willing to pay a high price if they view your product or service as having the greatest value, you can strategically create *price elasticity*—the responsiveness to changes in price of a good or service. If you increase your margins, you'll also have more money to invest in growing your business and marketing. As business growth expert Paul Lemberg says:

> *"Whoever obtains a wider margin per sale wins because of the resulting growth acceleration. Whoever aims for the low end of the pricing spectrum has a smaller margin and less money after paying bills for marketing."*

Why Competing on Price is Dangerous

Let's look back in retail history. Before Walmart, there was Kmart. Before Kmart, there was Ames. Before Ames, there was Woolworth's. Before Woolworth's, an ever-changing cast of regional discount retailers attempted to compete on price. However, as each rose in dominance, a new competitor came along with a new and lower *low price position*.

Recent years could be called the era of Walmart. The company seemed unstoppable and was considered the bane of competitors and vendors alike. Walmart consistently undercut competitors' low-price claims and used (and still uses) its market position as leverage to demand its vendors cut their margins to the bone. Then came a deep recession and rise of "dollar stores" such as Family Dollar and Dollar Tree. A 2011 study by WSL/Strategic

Retail[46] indicated that the more affluent shoppers have left Walmart because low prices weren't enough reason to stay.

~~~~

"Shoppers find unlimited inventories online, so they no longer worry about missing out if they don't buy an item in the store right now.

"So how can average retailers fight back?

"Here's the first tip: Low prices alone won't do it.

"So if you're not the biggest player in your space, what potential advantages do you have?

"Three things: loyalty, convenience and speed."

—Google, ZMOT[47]

~~~~

By continuously competing on price, Walmart has targeted its core shopper as a consumer who's highly price sensitive and has less money to spend as a result of the recession: "The core Walmart shopper can't pull Walmart out of this hole ... they don't have enough money to spend to reverse the decline."[48]

The study shows that 74 percent of Walmart's core shoppers go to dollar stores at least once a month, and 49 percent go several times each month. It also shows that 86 percent of Walmart shoppers no longer believe Walmart has the lowest prices.[49] As a press release describing the WSL/Strategic Retail report on Business Wire notes: "Every brick and mortar retailer lowered prices and shouted sales throughout the recession, while the Internet became the go-to place for shoppers in search of the

---

[46] WSL/Strategic Retail. "How America Shops: Where Did the Walmart Shopper Go?" 2011.

[47] Google. *ZMOT: Ways to Win Shoppers at the Zero Moment of Truth Handbook.* 2012.

[48] WSL/Strategic Retail. "How America Shops: Where Did the Walmart Shopper Go?" 2011.

[49] Business Wire. "Walmart's Reign as Price King is Over According to New 'How America Shops' Report: Survey Reveals Walmart Shoppers Finding Lowest Prices Elsewhere." August 3, 2011. [Available from: http://www.businesswire.com/news/home/20110803006332/en/Walmarts-Reign-Price-King-America-Shops-Report]

lowest price." In fact, the report describes Walmart's dilemma by asking: "So now what? If Walmart no longer stands for EDLP [Everyday Low Prices], what does Walmart stand for?"

Looking at the market for low-priced retailers, I have to ask: Have we hit bottom yet? The answer is no. If a company can come along and undercut Walmart's prices, easily convincing a vast majority of its core shoppers to leave, how can a sustainable business be built solely on *low price position?* I argue that it can't.

Consider the difference between Nordstrom and Walmart. The latter cuts prices to the bone, while pushing its vendors and suppliers to keep prices as low as possible. In fact, Walmart's strong-arm tactics have caused the company to receive bad publicity. Walmart also offers minimal customer service and a buying environment that's like a neon-lit warehouse.

By contrast, Nordstrom continually seeks ways to enhance customer service. It features warm and inviting stores, strong vendor relationships, and a substantial *price point.*

Blackberry and Apple technology companies provide a similar comparison. The Blackberry was once the dominant smartphone, but it has precipitously fallen in popularity as new product releases failed due to limited capabilities of its mobile operating system.[50]

Meanwhile, Apple continues to create better *value* by improving its iPhone and iPad. Apple's products are often the most expensive options, appearing to have one of the highest price points in the consumer electronics industry (44.4 percent profit margin generally[51], with reports of up to 58 percent on iPhones[52]). This positioning has made Apple one of the most profitable companies ever.

Not only does competing on price squeeze profit margins, but it produces dire consequences. Marlene Jensen, CEO of Pricing Strategy

---

[50] Rocha, E. "Blackberry Shares Jump After Bernstein Upgrades Stock." February 4, 2013. [Available from: http://www.reuters.com/article/2013/02/04/us-blackberry-shares-idUSBRE9130K120130204]

[51] Forbes. "Apple Inc: Ratios and Returns." 2013. [Available from: http://finapps.forbes.com/finapps/jsp/finance/compinfo/Ratios.jsp?tkr=AAPL]

[52] Oldroyd, C. "Apple Makes Twice the Profit Margins on US iPhone Sales as it Does iPad." July 27, 2012. [Available from: http://www.imore.com/apple-makes-huge-profit-margins-us-iphone-sales-ipad-only-half-good]

Associates and author of *Setting Profitable Prices*, *Pricing Psychology Report* and *The Tao of Pricing*, elaborates:

> *"Even if your competitor cannot beat you in a price war, you will still lose, even if you win. That's because at the end of the price war, your customers will believe your product is worth a lot less—due to that nice new extremely low price you've allowed them to pay—and you won't be able to raise the price all the way back up."*

Discounting Carries Risks

Continually relying on discounts carries similar risks. If a business discounts its products or services, many consumers conclude that the company:

- Has cheapened the products or services to remain profitable at the discount,
- Is about to come out with a newer and better version,
- Has discovered a problem with the product or service and needs to unload it,
- Has found that consumers who bought the product or service don't like it,
- Overpriced the product or service to begin with, or
- Is about to go out of business.

Consider human nature. The majority of consumers will perceive a higher level of risk involved with discounted prices, and this perceived risk intensifies nearly in proportion to how deep the discount is.

I've learned this in my own business, plus it's supported by compelling research by Ronald Drozdenko, Ph.D., professor and chair of Ancell School of Business Marketing Department at Western Connecticut State University.[53] He states: "There's considerable research on the price-quality relationship dating back several decades. A number of interpretations are given for this relationship, but I think it relates to risk reduction ... When

---

[53] Jensen, R.D.M., "Pricing Strategy and Practice: Risk and Maximum Acceptable Discount Levels." *Journal of Product & Brand Management*, 2005. 14(4): p. 264-270.

faced with little information or personal knowledge about a product, consumers tend to base a purchase on the most salient characteristic, which often is price. By the way, marketers know this and will increase prices beyond a necessary margin to establish this quality perception."

Think of it this way: If you see a bottle of wine you've never tried on sale for a 50 percent discount at the liquor store, you may consider that product inferior. Would you share that bottle with good friends at an important dinner party? Now consider the brand placed next to it on the shelf. It comes from a micro-distillery with its price 20 to 30 percent higher than most other brands. What's your perception of the quality of *that* wine? Much greater!

Back to Apple, a company that deeply understands the dangers of competing on price. It rarely, if ever, discounts its products. In fact, Apple's laptops are considerably more expensive when compared to a PC model with similar features. The company has created an elevated perception of quality in the design of its laptops as well as in the packaging, service, and support it offers. How would consumer perception change if, all of a sudden, Apple started deep discounting on some of its laptops packaged inside skimpy brown cardboard boxes?

Margin Analysis: Do the Math

Consider the wine choice example and the effects on profit margin from lowering price versus increasing value and price.

Suppose you produce the high-priced wine and you put a lot of effort into creating a high-quality product that holds substantial value for the consumer. It's packaged and marketed in a sharp way. It sells well, but you wonder how much more money you could make if you expanded your customer base. Perhaps you could reduce the price of your wine to pick off mid-range wine buyers who may believe your product is too expensive.

Currently, you charge $30 for a bottle that costs $15 to produce and ship—a healthy margin and probably far higher than in reality. So you decide to lower your price to $25—a 16 percent discount—to pull customers from slightly lower-priced competitors. All of your costs remain the same or continue to edge upward (labor, insurance, rent, utilities, etc.).

At $30 a bottle, you grossed $3,000 for every 100 bottles sold and made a profit of $1,500. However, at $25 a bottle, you will gross $2,500 for every 100 bottles and only make $1,000 profit. This means that, to break even, you have to sell an additional 20 bottles, thus increasing sales by 20 percent.

~~~~

"The effects of coupons, sales and discounts are exactly the same as cocaine. The first time you get a discount card in the mail you are elated! Wow! 10% off, 20% off, 2-for-1! You might rush out to the store and take advantage of the offer. But next time you drive by that store you think, I'll just wait and see if there are any more coupons coming. Next time you drive by that store you get mad since you forgot the coupon. Eventually you refuse to step into the store without a coupon."[54]

—Laura Ries, focusing consultant

~~~~

But additional sales at a lower price point aren't guaranteed because your current customers are wondering why you dropped the price all of a sudden. And your competitors—at the lower price point as well as your former price point—may react by discounting their products to compete against you. Will you discount your product again to continue growing your customer base? If so, you'll need to increase your sales even more to break even.

Let's go the other direction. Suppose you want to grow your price point instead while maintaining or increasing demand for your product. You can do this by adding greater value to the product. Say you'd like to increase the price by $5 to $35 a bottle. For every 100 bottles sold, you'd gross $3,500 and bring in $2,000 in profit—a 25 percent increase over the old price. This requires adding value to the product without increasing costs.

---

[54] Ries, Laura. "Coupons, Groupon and Cocaine" in blog "Ries' Pieces: On the Business of Branding." 2010.

Clearly, even a slight price reduction can wreak havoc on your profit margins. Meanwhile, the slightest uptick in price can put your business in a different growth mode. Even if you have to increase production costs by a dollar or two a bottle, you still come out ahead and can grow sales by positioning your product as a premium wine backed by an emotionally compelling story and a *Unique Advantage Point*. [55]

Value Perception Creates Price Elasticity

I've seen the results of price elasticity in my own business and with my clients. For example, I discussed a unique information service with Tom Trush of Write Way Solutions, a talented direct response copywriter, author of *The "You" Effect*, and member of the Predictable Profits Insiders' Club. During our brainstorming session, I read through his product materials and thought he had an excellent concept. Then I asked about price. At $47 a month, I thought he was significantly underpricing it. I also thought this price would undermine his clients' perception of the quality of the product, so I encouraged him to more than double it to $97 a month. At first he thought I was crazy, but changed his mind, saying:

> *"Earlier, I'd look at the competition and think, 'Well, they're doing this at X so I might as well do it at X, and if I go a little lower than the competition, it will make my offering look like a better deal or value.'*
>
> *"So when you told me to jump my fee, it made me extremely nervous. Naturally, I was thinking about my competitors and comparing my price to theirs. However, I've come to realize this is a dangerous thing to do.*
>
> *"In the end, I gained twice the profitability while doing the same work. A few people have told me the price was too high, but I'm not concerned with them because I'm targeting a high-end demographic. Also, now that I'm sharing the results my clients have had with this product, I think demand will continue to rise."*

Does Trush believe the increased fee helped boost the perceived quality of the offer?

---

[55] See Chapter 3.

"For sure. My challenge is continuing to provide unique insights to my clients that keep the perception high, but I enjoy this challenge."

More Examples of Value Perception

One of the most common objections I hear is this: *If I raise my prices, demand will fall off a cliff.* So let me give you more examples.

One of my clients offered a newsletter that proved incredibly valuable to his clients as indicated by the success stories. Although he was selling it as a monthly program for around $50, I estimated his average client was receiving more than 10 times the return from this investment (often much more). I immediately saw the discrepancy between the value of the product and the price, so I encouraged him to increase the price to $200 a month. He couldn't understand why people would pay that much and worried he would lose all his customers. To help ease his concerns, I explained how he'd created an exceptionally powerful *value perception,* which in turn created *price elasticity.*

When creating his set of products, he focused accurately on the needs and desires of his niche market to deliver a highly effective solution. He also positioned himself as a *trusted advisor,* which helped differentiate him and his products. The result? By increasing the price of his product, he attracted *more* customers and quickly saw a five-digit increase in his profits.

I helped another client increase his product's price point from $1,997 to $2,495, making him one of the most expensive competitors in his industry. Because we articulated its value so well, people were happy to pay the higher price, and his profits increased by 25 percent almost immediately. In fact, the marketing campaign I created for him generated more than $1.1 million *within 10 days* and exponentially more in the ensuing months.

Another client increased his average engagement from $2,500 a day to $15,000 a day (and I'm still arguing that this figure can go much higher). Because this particular company regularly produces a return on investment in the hundreds of thousands of dollars (often millions), most of his customers didn't blink an eye after announcing the price increase.

The value perception discussion that follows explains how to articulate the value, advantage, benefit, and experience you offer.

The Value Perception

When people see the *price* compared to the *value* of doing business, you want them to believe you're selling money at a discount. This creates the *value perception*. It might work for you to raise your prices *somewhat* without doing anything else. However, raising prices without also offering differentiating value and making sure your customers perceive that extra value could be a dangerous game.

Studies have shown that raising prices send a powerful psychological message to consumers. As pricing strategist and new business expert Marlene Jensen writes: "As consumers we have learned that the higher the value of a product, the higher it will be priced. A Mercedes is a better car than a Toyota. A Rolex is better than a Timex. Armani clothing is better than Sears … [If] someone is quoting $10,000 for a project and another person quotes $5,000, all that previous consumer training we've all had— that higher prices mean higher quality—can't help but enter the buyer's brain."[56]

Professor Drozdenko conducted a study in which he measured the effect on perceptions of quality and price for four products: sunglasses, perfume, computers, and tomato sauce. In all four product areas, he found that a higher price equated to a higher perception of quality by consumers. The highest increase was perfume at 21 percent, and the lowest was tomato sauce with an increase of 8 percent.

~~~~

"Consumers usually do not see your prices as a complete surprise. They may already have a rough idea of what your price is, or at least what prices for your type of product/service generally run. This is called an internal reference price."[57]

—Marlene Jensen, pricing strategist
and new business expert

~~~~

---

[56] Jensen, M. *Pricing Psychology Report: Price Changes You Can Make Today to Increase Cash.* 2004: Jensen-Fann Publishers.

[57] Jensen, M. *46 Ways to Raise Prices … Without Losing Sales.* 2005: Jensen-Fann Publishers. p. 134.

To reliably convince clients and customers the worth of your higher pricing, be crystal clear about why your product or service is superior to your competition. Most of your potential customers already have an idea what they should get in return for a certain amount of money so you have to convey a powerful value perception.

Think of Bergeron with his circuit board repair business (described in Chapter 5). He operates in a highly commoditized market so most people seeking his services have a price expectation based on what they've paid in the past. Typically, they expect to receive a properly repaired circuit board in a reasonable amount of time with a limited two-year warranty.

However, when customers come to Bergeron, they experience something completely different. He offers a topnotch repair, a loaner part so the equipment can remain online and productive, a lifetime warranty for each piece of equipment repaired, fast turnaround time, and much more. With an already huge value to the customer, he includes the assurance that customers will never have to pay for that type of repair on that piece of equipment again. Bergeron's price, at 35 percent higher than other repair companies, carries a greater *value perception*. As a result, customers believe they're buying money at a discount!

The key: If you're thorough in informing consumers about the *value* they're getting, they don't focus as much on price, as Professor Drozdenko notes:

> *"When consumers have more information about a product, such as past experience, consumer report ratings, information from peers, etc., then the price becomes a less important factor in the decision process."*

I would add that your marketing efforts play an important role, which is why I focus on identifying your niche, becoming a *trusted advisor,* and establishing your *Unique Advantage Point.* These all communicate value to the consumer. *The Growth Factor* and *value proposition* also ensure you're developing highly satisfied customers. This, in turn, increases referrals, word-of-mouth advertising, positive consumer reviews, and the like.

~~~~

"Encouraging consumers to take a price-oriented, statistical, rational approach to purchasing decisions can have disastrous unintended consequences. That's because contrary to popular opinion our emotions provide valuable insight. They steer us: A conservative estimate is that 95% of people's thought activity isn't fully conscious, and hence is intuitive and operating in the realm of emotion."[58]

—Dan Hill, President of Sensory Logic, Inc.

~~~~

Consider: results from management consulting company IPA's database of 880 marketing campaigns show that emotion-oriented campaigns generate twice as much profitability as traditional, hard-sell, reasoning-oriented campaigns.[59]

Articulating Your Value Perception

Be careful. You don't want to come out and state "here's the value you should perceive." But you can't assume potential buyers know that; they often don't realize what they're getting. So be sure you spell it out to them beforehand as you educate them on the benefits of your product or service. Articulate well how it will improve their lives or businesses, solve their problems, and give them a good return on their investment.

Then, after they purchase from you, remind them of how you're committed to helping them achieve the best possible result. You can do this by, for example, providing additional services or support and making it easy for them to contact you. You can also create a user manual and/or YouTube videos that demonstrate how to get the most out of what you

---

[58] Hill, D. "Your Brand Offers—and Your Company." 2010. [Available from: http://www.marketingprofs.com/articles/2010/4015/seven-reasons-why-leading-with-price-will-kill-your-advertising-your-branded-offersand-your-company]

[59] Hill, D. "Seven Reasons Why Leading With Price Will Kill Your Advertising, Your Branded Offers and Your Company." 2010. [Available at: http://www.marketingprofs.com/articles/2010/4015/seven-reasons-why-leading-with-price-will-kill-your-advertising-your-branded-offersand-your-company#ixzz2KbuePcQF]

offer. These touches also make clients aware of other products or services you offer and how these items can also improve their lives.

Work Within Your Market Range

Generally, you can't price far outside of the market range because people can't or won't pay more than what they believe is reasonable for the solution they seek. Therefore, you want to hit a sweet spot, usually at or toward the high end of the price range in your market, without pricing beyond the value you offer. But realize that, if you're too much of an outlier, people can't rationalize the cost for your service or product.

Examples abound in which the perceived quality of a product allowed its price to exceed the general price range. For example, the CEO of Starbucks, Howard Shultz, applied the value perception brilliantly to a cup of Starbucks coffee. Apple computers are priced far outside the price range for PCs. And you'll find more extreme examples, such as the price difference between any Rolls Royce and a high-end Toyota or a Rolex and even a high-end Timex.

Then there's the C6 Pizza made by Vancouver-based Steveston Pizza Company. Topped with lobster, black Alaskan cod, and a spoonful of Russian Osetra caviar, this pizza costs $450. Although Steveston may not sell a lot of C6 pizzas, offering such a luxury item increases the overall perception of quality for the rest of the pizzas.[60]

Create Targeted Add-Ons

In a more grounded example, think about Bergeron and the equipment repair services he offers. His price for this premium service falls outside the range charged by his competitors, but because he offers a lifetime guarantee, his clients believe it's a good deal.

Bergeron also understands that when his customers' equipment goes offline, their productivity declines, which cuts into their profits. That's why he offers loaner parts, which not only keep his customers' equipment run-

---

[60] [Available from: http://www.foxnews.com/leisure/2012/06/13/pricey-pie-450-pizza-includes-lobster-caviar/]

ning, but add to his bottom line. He knows the cost of his services is far less than the cost of replacing the entire piece of the equipment.

With these insights in mind, Bergeron understands his clients' price tolerance, so he creates targeted value-adds to increase their *value perception*. In turn, he can charge more and make a higher margin, which allows him to spend more than his competitors on developing and marketing his services.

IBM did this with its mainframe computer business. As Marlene Jensen notes in her book *46 Ways to Raise Prices ... Without Losing Sales,* IBM mainframe computers have always been more expensive than competitors' computers. However, the company understands its customers pay far less for computers than many other items. In addition, it knows that if a computer goes down, the cost to the company can be immense, especially for Internet-based retailers. To address this, IBM offers the fastest service response times and a replacement computer until the problem is fixed.

What does this mean? IBM and Bergeron sell more than a product or service; they sell security (e.g., a *Unique Advantage Point*). Certainly, then, opportunities exist to break the rules and get outside the price frame to increase your margin. However, as Lemberg warns, "You can go outside the range, but you need a reason for it."

Therefore, when you set price, be strategic about it. Price can help elevate you above the sea of *me-too competitors* and increase profits predictably—*if* you deliver the greatest value, advantage, benefit, and experience to your target market.

Strategies for Raising Prices

Chronically, entrepreneurs underprice their products or services due to reasons ranging from lack of business experience to believing their product isn't worth more money. Perhaps the most common reason involves failing to understand what people are willing to pay.

What does this mean for the market? Prices generally stay low. In fact, Tom Trush's example of underpricing his new offering shows that people can leave a significant amount of money on the table.[61] Of course, Tom is not alone. In my own business, I still find areas in which the price-to-value ratio is significantly unbalanced and may require an increase in price.

When I work with clients in similar situations, we look at their offerings and research their market. Then we develop a plan for raising prices that doesn't shock buyers but does allow the product to approach full value. After we get prices closer to full value, we seek ways to grow the *value perception* and increase the *price point* even further. Clearly, it's not just about increasing margins, but also finding ways to focus on *The Growth Factor* and add value. This can involve improving the service or product, adding services or value, and/or spending more time educating people on why they're receiving the greatest value, advantage, benefit, and experience.

Looking at Walter Bergeron's company again, he first raised the price for his service in a haphazard way. He knew he needed to increase his margins so he could gain the breathing room to create new offerings. Recognizing he was selling in a highly commoditized market, he had to be creative about change. But first he sought to generate the opportunity for change, as he explains:

> *"In the beginning, we knew we were trying to compete with everyone else based on pricing because we simply didn't know any better. So raising prices was an arbitrary move, but we intuitively knew we could charge more. Also, it was a test to see what would happen. As it turned out, we had no loss of clients, and we dramatically increased profits.*
>
> *"Then we decided if we did it again, we'd do it strategically. That's when we came up with the platinum-level program. This higher level of service differentiated us from everyone else and added a lot of value to the service we offer. We called attention to it and made a big deal out of it.*
>
> *"This program came out of asking our customers what their needs are. We had long talks with them and sent surveys asking what they want in a repair service. We realized how valuable a lifetime warranty would be for them, so we created value based on their needs, not an arbitrary stacking of*

---

[61] In addition to Tom's many talents, he also wrote a book called *The "You" Effect*. I highly recommend you read it.

services. As a result, what we offered became even more valuable to our customers than the thirty-five percent increase in price."

Tying Price to Performance

It's smart to address the risk customers may perceive in higher prices by offering a guarantee. For example, I had a client who paid me over $720,000; a cost that would normally cause hesitation. However, I shifted the risk perception by tying my fee to performance. In this way, I put "skin in the game" by assuming all of the risk of working with me and receiving the bulk of my payment as a percentage of the profits I earned the company. With the windfall of profits they earned because of my contribution, they didn't blink an eye when they paid me nearly three-quarters of a million dollars. I've structured my model to only get paid *after* they get paid. That puts the onus on me to perform.

Zappos does a variation of this, too. By offering a 365-day return policy and free return shipping, the company negates the customer's risk of buying shoes online. If customers don't like the shoes they order, they get their money back at no expense to them.

Kevin Hallenbeck with Sandler Training makes this important point:

"The question is: Can you add value and do it efficiently? If you move your price point up but it takes three times as long to sell, you need to consider the associated cost. You can't move the price point up without adding value, and cost is involved in that, too. Or you could be aggressive in some other way.

"There's no single answer, and that's the challenge in business and why market research matters. If there's no need, you're out of luck because no one will want your product or service. And if you don't uncover hidden costs and adjust accordingly, you'll also be out of luck."

Strategies for Increasing Profits

Entrepreneurs can miss opportunities to make simple changes to increase profits. That means you might find a lot of low-hanging fruit if you look for it.

Here, I've listed 11 strategies my clients have found helpful. (You'll recognize a few from previous examples.) Also refer to Marlene Jensen's *46 Ways to Raise Prices ... Without Losing Sales* for inspiration.

1. Break your service down into component parts and charge for each component (if this creates a margin advantage).
2. Add a parallel service or product at a high margin that increases the value of the original service or product.
3. Create a premium package of products or services and offer it as a high-value alternative (but only if it creates a margin advantage).
4. Offer upgrades to your products or services.
5. Offer consulting around a product to help customers gain maximum value.
6. Establish the return on investment (ROI) so clients can see the cost as a small percentage of the value received.
7. Reposition a slightly updated version to a luxury or higher-value category (e.g., go from mid-range up one level).
8. Test new pricing strategies on various market segments and optimize those that promise the best results.
9. Reposition the selling point in your advertising so that, rather than selling a product or service, you're selling security.
10. Increase your price to the next psychological hurdle (e.g., $8 to $8.99 per unit or $120 per hour to $125).
11. Offer a low introductory price (e.g., basic cable TV service at $24.60 a month), then escalate the price for additional or premium-level services (e.g., premium cable TV for $127.40 a month).

So far, we've discussed fundamental ways to identify your core market and craft a compelling *value proposition* for prospective buyers. The next section examines the tactical logistics of bringing them in and building a powerful, long-term relationship through your marketing promotions.

SECTION IV:
PROMOTION—THE THREE
PHASES OF MARKETING:
DATING, ENGAGEMENT, MARRIAGE

Chapter 7:
Dating—The Art of Attracting Customers

"Direct marketing is the business of acquiring customers and getting to know them—keeping track of their transactions with you and then continuing to delight them by serving their needs, creating new wants and, above all, persuading them to act."[62]

—Denny Hatch, direct response marketer

YOU DON'T HAVE to know all your clients personally to have a relationship, but you want them to feel as if they're personally important to you and your company. They need to know they matter, their business with you matters, and you care about making a difference in their lives.

The buyer/seller relationship follows a trajectory similar to that of two people meeting, falling in love, and then joining in marriage. For this reason, I've labeled the three phases of marketing/promotion: *dating, engagement,* and *marriage*.

~ ~ ~ ~

"We're entering an era of reciprocity. We now have to engage people in a way that's useful or helpful to their lives. The consumer is looking to satisfy their

---

[62] Jackson, D.H.D. *2,239 Tested Secrets for Direct Marketing Success.* 1998, Chicago: NTC Business Books, p. 358.

needs, and we have to be there to help them with that. To put it another way:
How can we exchange value instead of just sending a message?"[63]

—Kim Kadlec, Worldwide VP,
Global Marketing Group, Johnson & Johnson

~~~~

Dating represents approaching someone for the first time and introducing yourself in a compelling enough way that your prospect wants to
take the next step. *Dating* involves generating leads, developing prospects,
and convincing them to make that initial purchase with you. You do this in
a non-offensive way that's comfortable to the person and clearly demonstrates you offer a unique solution that delivers value. You treat your prospects with respect and, as an advocate for their interests, you present them
with a compelling offer that's difficult to refuse.

That means *dating* should never be about pressure tactics, taking advantage of someone's trust or vulnerability, or making a person feel
trapped. Instead, you engage them in questions to determine if what you
have fits for what's needed or desired.

Direct Response Marketing Versus Brand Marketing

Dating is also about *direct response marketing* as opposed to *brand marketing*. In
brand marketing, you use images, advertisements, catch phrases, and other
strategies to encourage the buying public to perceive your product or service through a certain lens. Examples: *Have a Coke and a Smile* or the
Goodyear Blimp appearing at important sporting events, or cuddly
cartoons, or a man and a woman running through an urban landscape with
the phrase *Just Do It.* However, *brand marketing* is rarely about getting someone to take action to learn more or buy the product. People rarely think,
Wow, those bears are funny. I think I'll get up off the couch and buy what they're selling.

By contrast, *direct response marketing* gets someone to take action, such as
providing personal information, contacting a sales associate, or even buying
the product. As leading direct response marketer Denny Hatch says:

---

[63] Google. ZMOT: *Ways to Win Shoppers at the Zero Moment of Truth Handbook.* 2012.

"Marketing is acquiring customers to increase your share of market and getting them to spend more with you to increase your share of wallet. Direct response marketing does this at a distance."

Direct response marketing has been around for approximately 500 years—ever since the first mail order catalogs were produced in Venice in the 1500s. By the 1600s, garden catalogs were available and, by the 1700s, they included woodcut pictures to encourage sales. Even before the American Revolution, Benjamin Franklin issued a book catalog seeking mail order sales.[64] To say the least, direct response marketing has had a long history of success.

In fact, this kind of marketing still leads to dramatic successes. My clients have experienced product launches and marketing campaigns that have garnered substantial profits. A recent product launch, for example, used the principles of direct response marketing to generate revenues of $250,000 in the first 24 hours and $1.125 million in ten days.

Direct response marketing works by inviting people into a sequenced sales process that involves two fundamental steps:

1. **Lead Generation:** In this initial step, you make a time-limited offer of valuable, risk-free, and helpful content (e.g., no charge, no obligation, no strings attached). In exchange, you collect names and contact information. You give away information that has high-perceived value and begin creating buzz for the product.

2. **Order Generation:** In the second step, you must nurture these interested people by educating them on your product or service. With this education, you position yourself as a trusted authority and your prospects are excited about your product or service. Only then will you make it available with a compelling offer. By adding value such as an expanded guarantee, you can entice your leads to act within a specific timeframe.

---

[64] Jackson, D.H.D. *2,239 Tested Secrets for Direct Marketing Success* 1998, Chicago: NTC Business Books. p. 358.

By contrast, *brand marketing* rarely makes the introduction (lead generation) and rarely, if ever, asks or impels the prospect to take action and grow the relationship (order generation). In dating terms, the brand marketer looks at the pretty woman but rarely introduces himself and never asks for a date. However, he does his best to look sharp and project a certain image.

One last difference: It's incredibly expensive and difficult to succeed at brand marketing, while it's far less expensive and much easier to succeed at direct response marketing. Why? With brand marketing, it's critical not only to come up with the necessary compelling image, logo, and catchphrase, but also to saturate the marketplace with ads. Plus, you have to do this over time and via a number of media such as TV, radio, magazines, the Internet, and so on. As an entrepreneur or small business owner with a limited budget, you'd find it financially impossible to mount such a sustained campaign. It would be tantamount to trying to fill the Grand Canyon by throwing bricks into its maw. You couldn't maintain the intensity and consistency necessary to affect the mindset of consumers in your marketplace.

Direct response marketing, on the other hand, is highly targeted and designed to generate a response within a tight timeframe. Results can be measured and tracked in terms of a specific advertisement or type of prospect. Ads can be run using any form of media, such as catalogs, Internet, print, radio, TV, telemarketing, mail, email, and much more, plus you can track the performance of each outlet you use.

Properly implemented direct response marketing can achieve results immediately or within a short amount of time. Rather than spend a lot of money building a brand image, you're focusing your resources on actions that will quickly generate income. Because this type of marketing creates trackable and measurable data, it can also be optimized. That means you can quickly terminate any marketing efforts that fall flat before they become expensive mistakes.

Direct response marketing thus offers entrepreneurs and small business owners a cost-effective means to introduce themselves to their market and incite action.

Direct Response Marketing in Action

In one successful campaign I designed, we laser-targeted the market for a new product. Initially, we offered the product "at cost" for a trial period so customers could get a sense of the possible results. If they liked it, we would charge them the full price after 30 days. If they returned it within the 30 days, they got their money back. This meant low risk to the consumer.

The campaign consisted of two letters sent via regular mail and three emails. To date, that campaign has paid well over six figures and still generates income a year and a half later. And because the people who bought the product have experienced great results with it, we've up-sold additional products to them and increased the lifetime customer value.

Fred Catona is founder and CEO of Bulldozer Digital, the first ad agency to specialize in direct response radio advertising. Catona has successfully guided the launches of Priceline.com and FreeCreditReport.com. About the power of direct response marketing, he says:

> *"With Priceline.com, in one hundred and twenty days, sixty-five percent of the country recognized the brand because we did a lot of advertising. It was strictly radio with actor William Shatner carrying the message.*
>
> *"Now, a lot of people say you can't build brand and make sales simultaneously. Well, in that same period, we probably did two hundred million dollars in sales. So direct response marketing works, and it will become stronger and stronger."*

Create an Ascension Ladder

Despite the speed with which both Catona and I have achieved results, we don't rely on pressure tactics or leap too quickly to make the sale. Instead, I suggest creating an *ascension ladder* with your direct response marketing campaigns. Rather than introduce yourself and then push hard for the sale, say hello and offer value to build relationships and/or allow prospects to try your product in a low-risk way.[65] That's the beginning of the *ascension ladder*. As you move upwards with seminars, coaching, and consulting, the investment increases. When you deliver such extraordinary value at every step in your ladder, your customers will want more of you. Using *ascension ladders* will increase three things: sales, retention, and the lifetime value of your customer.

When you look at Tony Robbins's business model from a 30,000-foot view, you'll see his blog and book at the first level. Then you'll see his home study programs followed by his "Unleash the Power Within" seminar (and others). Mastery University follows from the seminar, then his Platinum Partnership and, finally, working with Tony one-on-one for a fee of $1,000,000 a year and a percentage of your increased profits. Clearly, Tony has built quite an empire with this model. You can too.

Once trust and authenticity have been established, you can move your prospects up the *ascension ladder*.

~~~~

"According to a recent analysis of more than 500 B2B companies, proper follow-up to marketing-generated leads occurs less than 25% of the time."[66]
—Marketing Leadership Council

~~~~

With my own clients, we typically introduce prospects to a product trial, available to use for a limited amount of time at a low price. In some cases, we even give them the product free in either a beta test or a limited free-trial offer. We've already identified those most likely to be hungriest for the solution; they see a small initial investment for a trial as low risk and worth trying. When we deliver the value we promise, they'll likely continue doing business with us.

---

[65] You see the *ascension ladder* in action by registering at http://www.PredictableProfitsPlaybook.com, and joining our exclusive membership newsletter called: The Predictable Profits Insiders' Club.
[66] *Marketing Leadership Council.* 2008. [cited 2012; Available from: https://mlc.executiveboard.com/Public/Merchandisers/MLC%20Value%20of%20the%20Membership.pdf]

Because we strive to create a product or service that offers high value, more often than not, customers or clients have an exceptionally positive experience, which convinces them to purchase. We can then take them further up the *ascension ladder* by making a higher-value offer to help them achieve even greater results. At every rung on the ladder, we give them more of what they want at ever-increasing value.

Throughout the process, we work to build trust and minimize risk. Isn't that what you want when you're dating?

~~~~

"On average, organizations that nurture their leads experience a 45% lift in lead generation ROI over those organizations that do not ... By nurturing leads with relevant content ... organizations can effectively encourage the right buyers to engage with Sales at the right time, and improve overall lead generation ROI."[67]

—Benchmark Report

~~~~

Measure, Verify, and Test

When I asked Denny Hatch to specify the three key differences between exceptional and marginal direct response marketing, he said, "Arithmetic, arithmetic, and arithmetic!" He's referring to the necessity to track, measure, verify, and test how well your marketing efforts perform.

By including markers (e.g., unique and track-able coupon codes, URLs, call-in numbers, offers, datasets, etc.) in your marketing campaigns using different media—print, radio, TV, mail, email, and more—you can track which media and which advertisement generates the most business. So when someone takes action, you can identify the specific marketing piece, advertisement, or media and the time each piece was sent.

Keep an eye on these metrics for each marketing piece in each area of the media:

---

[67] *Benchmark Report: 2012 Lead Generation: Key Trends for Generating Leads of the Highest Quality.* 2012.

- Response rate (Total number of people who responded to the advertisement)
- Inquiry to lead conversion rate (Traffic divided by number of leads captured)
- Cost per lead (Cost divided by number of leads)
- Sale conversion rate (Total number of leads divided by total number of sales)
- Average buyer value (Total dollar amount of sales divided by total number of buyers)

You can also add markers for tracking individual elements of a pitch, doing this by media type. For example, the photo in pitch A is working better than the photo in pitch B when the ad runs in a magazine. However, response drops when photo A runs on a billboard or in newsprint. Or a certain piece of text or tagline works well in general interest magazines, but response falls when it's used in trade magazines or magazines targeted to men, women, certain professions, or particular interests.

By tracking, measuring, verifying, and testing your marketing, you can then drop the pieces that aren't working well and optimize those that are. A dollar spent on a highly effective marketing effort can generate a return that's 10, 20, 30, or even 100 times the original investment.

I often ask new coaching clients what's working for them and what isn't. Generally, they'll identify what they believe has been a significant driver of business for them, but when I ask why, they can't explain. Despite the importance of measuring and testing, they have no method for proving what's working or not—and why.

If you look at the advertising in your local media, you'll see most have no more content than a business card with the company's name, motto, what they do, and perhaps an offer for a discount on a product or service. Often, these companies don't know how well the ad works or what could be improved to increase the leads and business it generates. Most of them only know the competition does it, and they suspect business would drop off if they didn't run the ad. However, if they had a tracking mechanism or marker built in—e.g., a particular phone number or coupon tied to that ad—they could tell if people are responding to it and then figure out how to optimize it.

~~~~

"Half the money I spend on advertising is wasted. The trouble is I don't know which half."

—John Wanamaker, department-store
magnate in the late 1800s

~~~~

Testing Means More Money for You
It's not enough to merely track results; you're advised to test different direct response marketing efforts for several reasons.

First, if you test two or more offers or ads on a small subset of your market, you can see which one is more effective before issuing it to the entire market. As mentioned, you can also test individual elements of an ad or pitch, such as a photo, placement of text, color, punctuation, font, messaging, and so forth. This helps you create the most effective pitch.

Even tiny details can produce phenomenal results. Anne Holland of Anne Holland Ventures, Inc. and WhichTestWon.com has witnessed this time and again. She says:

"We often see even the smallest detail making a huge difference in determining which ad is more effective. I remember a test in which someone used a colon between two words in one ad and a dash in another. The email using a colon had a twelve percent increase in clicks! I thought, wow, that little dinky thing has so much effect.

"In another interesting test, a chain of fitness clubs ran advertising all over London and other cities in the U.K. For the whole campaign, they used a particular picture of a happy customer at the gym as their model.

"Near the end of the campaign after the big broadcast media had run, they tossed in a smaller online campaign. They had a guy who loves testing, so he said let's try other models and see which one does best. It turns out the model they hired for the giant, expensive campaign tested worse than the one for the smaller online campaign. Both models were good-looking men, but one

was in his late twenties and one was in his fifties. The fifty-something model 'won.' The fitness centers spent a lot of money using a model who didn't work well. If they'd run the photo test first, they would've gotten much more bang for their buck."

~~~~

"There are two rules in Direct Response Marketing, and two rules only. Rule No. 1: Test everything. Rule No. 2: See rule No.1."

—Malcolm Decker,

copywriter/designer/creative consultant

~~~~

Early in my career, the direct response marketing pieces I created had such gangbuster results that I believed I could walk on water. Then along came my good friend Jerry. He was new to the field of marketing and copywriting, and I was coaching him. For fun, he suggested we have a little competition. I agreed. We would each pick a product that pays an affiliate commission, write copy to advertise it, then see who generates the most sales.

So I created a skillfully designed website and textbook salescopy. I liked it. According to all standards, it looked like a winner. By comparison, with no technical expertise, Jerry created a rudimentary website that was thrown together in minutes, and his copy violated every rule in the book. I would have bet a million dollars I'd outsell Jerry 10:1.

However, when put to the test, his website brought in more sales than mine. For the life of me, I couldn't figure it out. But it became one of my best learning experiences. Why did I lose this contest? Well, in this particular market space, what I'd created looked too much like *marketing*, whereas Jerry's website conveyed a message like he was speaking from personal experience. What I liked didn't matter. *I am not my customer.*

Diversifying a Must

I know a guy who writes for a living. As a freelancer, he's always looking for ways to guarantee a steady stream of work without having to spend much time vying for new jobs. One day, he did a project for a huge technology company. The person who hired him liked his work and offered him more. Before long, he had a steady stream of business coming in and thought he'd never have to compete for new clients again.

Then the economy went into free fall and shed as many as 500,000 jobs a month, his lucrative client battened down the hatches and stopped spending money. My friend thought he'd survive by being like a mouse on a luxury liner; his income was small potatoes compared to the resources of this behemoth company.

But he was wrong. Approximately one week after the company shut off all nonessential spending, he found himself with no work whatsoever. Established projects were cancelled and new projects evaporated. That left him without any source of income during the worst economic crash in 70 years.

This may be an extreme example, but it illustrates you can't safely rely on one source of revenue or one method of generating revenue. You have to diversify.

Early in my own career, I was generating $26,000 a month in commissions from a client for a lead generation strategy I created.[68] Unfortunately, because I focused solely on one strategy—Pay Per Click advertising—it left me vulnerable.

For well over a year, my strategy worked well for this client, we were both happy, and I assumed this approach would continue to work. Then Google changed its algorithm and my commission fell by almost two-thirds. Within another few months, it dwindled to just $1,500 a month. But if I had generated additional strategies before Google changed its algorithm, this wouldn't have happened. I chalk this up to another one of life's humbling lessons.

Despite how obvious this may seem after the fact, I'm always surprised how many entrepreneurs and small business owners rely on only one or two sources of generating business. Technology changes (e.g., telephone books), laws change (e.g., Do Not Call List), rules change (e.g., Pay Per Click Advertising), algorithms change (e.g., Search Engine Optimization)

---

[68] On occasion, I will accept private clients who are in good standing with The Predictable Profits Insiders' Club. Once I accepted, I get paid only if my clients succeed, and the amount I'm paid is based on their level of success—I'm that sure of the power of Predictable Profits.

and economies change. Far too many people believe they can thrive with 100 percent of their business coming from one source.

Not so. You must build a financial fortress around your business so you can sustain growth, even during the worst economies. Building this fortress requires recognizing two realities: (1) the environment can change, and (2) you must always look for additional business and revenue-generating opportunities.

The Money Wheel

When talking with clients about the need to have a diverse ecosystem of revenue generation strategies, I use the metaphor of a *Money Wheel*.

Now, for any wheel to provide a smooth and predictable ride, you need to have more than one or two spokes. Not only that, but each spoke does its job to provide a smooth ride. This points to the need to measure, test, and verify each spoke so you can understand how well each is working while identifying weak spokes that could be optimized to improve the ride.

Remember, during the *dating* phase of building customer relationships, you need enough lead generation and conversion strategies to guarantee a smooth, predictable ride. These strategies and tools can include:

- Email,
- Direct mail,
- Pay Per Click advertising,
- Periodic product launches,
- Radio, newspaper, and TV advertising,
- Online social networking,
- Strategic partnerships, and/or
- Enticements.

The *New Consumer* and Global Competition

Building your own *Money Wheel* may seem like a lot of effort, but it doesn't have to be. It takes a persistent daily or weekly strategy to move your business forward and find the portfolio of lead or income generating strategies that works for you. This can make the difference between being *good* and being *exceptional*. Why? Because you're doing what most entrepreneurs and small business owners won't do.

In my experience, the majority fails to recognize their competition no longer resides in the Yellow Pages or just down the street. With people now shopping online, consider your competitors to be global. And they're constantly jockeying for new customers, thinking about how they can grow their businesses and win over the hearts of *your* customers.

Remember, your buyer has changed also. In this *New Consumer* era, prospective customers have vast amounts of information at their fingertips and nearly limitless options. They'll spend their money, but their buying patterns have changed. You must adapt.

However, you may find it reassuring that 99.9 percent of entrepreneurs don't do what they could be doing to get business. That applies not only to entrepreneurial shops but to medium and large businesses, too.

~~~~

How can you stand out and make *predictable profits with your promotion?* By mastering three things: (1) *direct response marketing,* (2) the *ascension ladder* of dating, engagement, and marriage, and (3) the *money wheel.*

—Charles E. Gaudet II

~~~~

Generating Leads and Sales

Dating introduces you to those most hungry for your solution, and lead generation is the basis of that introduction. Let's delve more deeply into the specifics.

You want to interact with potential clients or customers in a way that's comfortable for them and allows you to quickly ascertain if they're good prospects for your solution. In cold sales, you'd first identify suspects and then engage in a form of discussion. This might be through cold calls, tradeshows, or responses to marketing materials (direct mail, email, social media, etc.). Through this interaction, you can quickly identify your prospects.

Once you do, you build trust and authenticity by offering value up front at no cost. Specifically, you want to make a low-risk free offer related to the solution the prospect is seeking. Additionally, this low-risk initial offer must have a high-perceived value—to a point you could actually charge for it. This will likely persuade the prospect to trade his or her contact information for the offer. In fact, you want the offer to be so compelling that the prospect says, "Yes, I'm interested and I want more information." As Bob Bly noted in his book *How to Create Irresistible Offers:* "Just by adding a free bait piece to your offer, you can often double the response to your ads and mailings over what the response for essentially the same offer would be without the free information offer."[69]

What's another good reason to initially give away something of value? It's a first opportunity to demonstrate the level of customer service a prospect can expect by doing business with you. For example, Turbo Tax allows people to use its online tax preparation service free to completely fill out their tax forms. Users can log off and leave the service at any time; there's no request to make a purchase until after they've finished preparing their taxes. Along the way, they're reminded of value-adds by Turbo Tax to increase the perceived value of the offer.

For Keith Lee, president of American Retail Supply, this concept forms a critical component of his personal success in sales and the success of the company he leads. In fact, this notion of initiating customer relationships with exceptional customer service right from the start was the impetus for his book, *Out-Nordstrom Nordstrom: Creating the World's Best Customer Service.* He wrote:

> *"One thing we believe is you need to give before you expect to get. For instance, if people go to our website and request our catalog, they get a whole lot more than our catalog. The first thing they see when they open the package from us is our book, Out-Nordstrom Nordstrom. We also offer information on green packaging, because that's big in our industry now, and information on many other resources we have for them, whether they buy from us or not.*

---

[69] Bly, R.W. *How to Create Irresistable Offers: The Easiest Way on Earth to Make Your Marketing Generate More Leads, Orders, and Sales.* 2009: American Writers & Artists, Inc.

"The first thing they see when opening the package is a note from me that says, 'The main reason I have sent my book Out-Nordstrom Nordstrom is because I want you to know this is the type of service you can expect from us here at American Retail Supply each and every time. If we should ever let you down, please call us right away at 800-426-5708 so we can make it right. If you're still not happy, please call me on my direct line, 253-859-7310. You may also find you can implement some of the ideas in the book in your own business …'

"What we want to do is give them high expectations right up front in terms of what they can expect from us in customer service."[70]

As Lee knows, you want your prospects to trust you and see you as an authentic provider of a unique solution.

Examples of powerful initial low-risk, high-value offers include white papers (awesome for B2B marketing as well as B2C), catalogs, samples, free trials, beta tests, needs assessments, diagnostics, free consultation, free demonstration, a webinar or teleseminar, consumer awareness guides, information kits, free audits, initial planning sessions, e-zines, seminars, trainings, CDs, DVDs, and more.

Why am I emphasizing the offer of free information? Because people today are inherently information seekers. They want to improve their lives, do their jobs better, make themselves happier, become richer, have greater sex appeal, live healthier, and have more freedom. Information draws them in. Kim Kadlec, Worldwide Vice President, Global Marketing Group, Johnson & Johnson says:

"… what needs to be top of mind for all marketers, no matter how established their brand is, is to stay relevant among our consumers.

"We have to think about how the lives of our end users are changing, whether that end user is a consumer, a patient, a doctor or anyone else. And to remain relevant we need to be a part of their new ecosystem."

---

[70] Lee, Keith. *Out-Nordstrom Nordstrom: Creating the World's Best Customer Service.* 2011.

Well-timed Enticements

Don't regard *dating* as selling. Rather, it's matchmaking and educating. Then once the connection happens, a well-timed enticement to take a next step, even make a purchase, follows. This enticement usually involves acting within a specific timeframe to gain relevant additional value—e.g., a reduced price, membership to a newsletter, product accessories, or an enhanced guarantee to reduce the risk of purchase.

~~~~

"If we engage Sales teams with our buyers too early, we risk losing the sale entirely. To succeed in this evolved market, it's more critical than ever to have an intricate understanding of our audience, our messaging, and our channels. When we understand our audience's needs and preferences, we create memorable communications experiences that will resonate and convert."[71]

—Benchmark Report

~~~~

Because this process ascends up the ladder, direct response marketing must gather information about the prospect as early as possible in exchange for something of value from you. It may seem obvious, but you want the name and contact information for *anyone* inside your target market. In addition, most people won't buy right away, so we need to follow up with them and strengthen the relationship by building trust and authenticity.

We don't want them to feel pressured, but we do want to be "on their minds" when they're ready to buy. By giving you contact information in exchange for something of value, they're essentially giving you permission to follow up. And this permission will remain intact as long as you're not too intrusive and strike the right balance between offering relevant, valuable information that builds trust and asking them to act. Denny Hatch describes the balance this way:

---

[71] *Benchmark Report: 2012 Lead Generation: Key Trends for Generating Leads of the Highest Quality.* 2012. [Excerpt available from:
http://www.meclabs.com/training/misc/12284_2012%20Lead%20Generation%20Benchmark%20Report%20-%20EXCERPT.pdf]

"In lead generation, you want the prospect to go on to the next step, and the next, and the next. The more you tell, the less you sell. If you talk too much, you could give the prospect a reason to say no. Every step of the lead generation process must be thought through thoroughly. At what point do you mention the product? Where in the series do you talk price?"

Again, if your motto is *I could sell ice to an Eskimo,* don't use this approach. You won't succeed with the *New Consumer.* He or she is one smart Eskimo who won't fall for pressure sales, manipulation, tricks, hucksters, and schemes.

Instead, success requires acknowledging that not every suspect will become a prospect as you work to generate leads. This not only saves you from wasting money on people who won't buy; it increases trust and the value of your brand while protecting your reputation.

Target and Qualify Carefully

Be selective. You want to invest in—and bring up the *ascension ladder*—only those people for whom your product or service offers the best solution. Hallenbeck makes the point this way:

"It's not so much that good salespeople qualify well, but that they disqualify quickly. If you're not a prospect of mine, the sooner I recognize that and move on, the better for both of us.

"Weak salespeople keep talking at you—whether in person such as on a salesroom floor or through email, cold calls, direct mail, or other forms of solicitations. They keep trying to sell you something. But if you're not a prospect, it's frustrating for both of you. If the suspect is cold and doesn't need ice cubes, it's the wrong zip code, so move on."

If you push a suspect into being a poorly qualified prospect and then push that prospect into something that isn't a good fit, you'll damage your credibility. Such customers are likely to share their dissatisfaction with friends and family and through social media. They don't like feeling fooled and taken advantage of. Most likely they'll view your product or service as an ineffective solution.

However, disqualifying suspects quickly doesn't mean you'll never be able to do business with them. You may not qualify them with your current offer, but they may be interested in future offers.

Writing a Message That Tells a Story

All good copywriting speaks to the needs and desires of prospects in a way that relates to their lives and makes clear how the solution you offer will better their lives.

Effective copywriting that tells a compelling story is exemplified in a legendary letter written by Bill Bonner. In 1978, Bill found himself with three failed business ventures and $70,000 in debt. Then he came up with an idea for a business based on a newsletter he created titled *International Living*. To launch the business, he wrote a letter to test his concept and sent it to a list of suspects. Here's the copy he wrote:

> *"You look out your window, past your gardener, who is busily pruning the lemon, cherry, and fig trees amidst the splendor of gardenias, hibiscus, and hollyhocks. The sky is clear blue. The sea is a deeper blue, sparkling with sunlight. A gentle breeze comes drifting in from the ocean, clean and refreshing as your maid brings breakfast in bed.*
>
> *"For a moment, you think you have died and gone to heaven.*
>
> *"But this paradise is real. And affordable. In fact, it costs only half as much to live this dream lifestyle as it would to stay in your own home!*
>
> *"Dear reader, I would like to send you a FREE copy of a unique and invaluable report. It's called the 5 Best Retirement Destinations in the World. And it tells you about the best places in the world for retirement living ... "[72]*

From this mailing on day one, Bonner turned a profit by capturing interest with a lead offer and making subsequent offers, taking new leads up the *ascension ladder*. This created the foundation of Agora, Inc., a $500

---

[72] Hatch, D. *Method Marketing: How to Make a Fortune by Getting Inside the Heads of Your Customers.* 1995: Bonus Books.

million direct response business with offices all around the world. All of this from the power of good copywriting!

The elements Bonner used are worth striving for in your own copy. Ask these questions to help produce compelling marketing pieces that get results:

- Are you marketing to people with a clear need or desire for your offer?
- Do your suspects/prospects have the financial resources and decision-making power to buy your offer?
- Why should your suspect/prospect engage in a relationship with you right now?
- What have you done to create desire?
- Do your suspects/prospects feel you truly understand their problem, need, and/or desire?
- Have you told them how their lives will be improved by your offer?
- Have you reduced their risk by providing free information with high perceived value?
- Have you shared information that helps the suspect/prospect learn something that's new and relevant?
- Are you working to create a relationship rather than pressure the suspect/prospect into a sale?
- Is the content so compelling that suspects/prospects will want to share it?

If you can answer these questions affirmatively, you're ready to deliver your message and ask for that first date.

Dating Campaign Examples

You'll find probably as many strategies for generating leads and developing prospects as there are businesses. As an example of what can be done in the *dating* phase, Walter Bergeron describes his Shock and Awe Campaign:

"Once we figure out which companies use this type of equipment, we send them a series of letters and emails, make phone calls, and involve as many types of media as we can. We even fax them. And then we send them short, niche-specific books that we've written.

"Once we identify those who have the budget and the equipment, they became our home-run customers—the guys we want to do business with. Knowing the value of certain prospects to us, we know we can spend a great deal of money to acquire their business. We try to pull them away from whatever they're doing now, be that buying new equipment or going to one of our repair competitors. We want to win them over, so we identify how much we can spend, and we go all out.

"That's where the video case comes into play. When the prospect opens the case, a small DVD screen begins to play a video that starts with a message from me and then goes into detail on our company. In the case, we also provide various materials and a genuine New Orleans King Cake for the prospect to enjoy while watching the video.

"This isn't a cheap alternative; it's expensive to do that, especially when you look at the entire campaign. We're spending almost five hundred dollars to do this, so it's important to stand out and not do what everyone else does. All of those things go into a long and complex campaign to generate and then convert that lead."

Bergeron puts the *ascension ladder, Money Wheel,* and concept of *direct response marketing,* plus innovation and more at work.

Another example comes from Panda Sunglasses, which makes high-end sunglasses with frames made from bamboo. For Luke Lagera, one of the three cofounders of Panda, his company's lead generation strategies have depended on telling a good story about the product and leveraging social and traditional media. As he says:

"We engage our audience through tradeshows, which is normally how fashion does it. You go to a tradeshow where they're looking for emerging brands, and they pick you up that way. Second to that is social media, promoting not only the product but the story behind the product.

"That story details how a bamboo sunglass company helped save a non-profit and we're now on the board of The TOMA Foundation. Basically, for every pair of sunglasses purchased, the Panda/TOMA partnership provides an eye or medical exam to a person in need, and we'll donate a pair of glasses as well. So there's a story behind the product, and that's what people buy into.

"Via emails and website, we keep people updated on our trips to Columbia and how we help people. That's what our business has turned into. It's not a shareholder mentality; it's a stakeholder mentality. How can you help the people you work for and who work for you? How can you help the environment and everything else so it's not only about maximizing margins?"

Panda's story of helping the poor gain access to eye and health care makes for a compelling argument for consumers: We offer a high-quality product, and the sooner you buy, the sooner you'll help the less fortunate. And the more pairs of sunglasses you buy, the more help you'll deliver to people in need.

It doesn't end there. The company was featured in *Entrepreneur, The Huffington Post, The Washington Post,* and others. Nordstrom also agreed to carry its product, which provided leverage while Panda was seeking relationships with other retailers. This opened a whole new level of sales, as Lagera explains:

"Entrepreneur magazine reached out and did an article on 'How does an emerging brand less than a year old end up on the shelves of Nordstrom?' That was a game changer. It helped spread our story and gave us the legitimacy and presence to go to other places—and for other places to hear about us and see that we have a legit story and a good brand.

"Now, when we solicit or pitch to new retailers, we come at them from the angle of, 'Your competitors are doing it; why aren't you?' Because Nordstrom has the sunglasses, we'll pitch to Neiman Marcus and Macy's. ABC Home in New York has them, and a similar company would be Tyler's brand in Texas. We tell new retail prospects that these stores have done it; here's our turnover on the product; here are our best products. We say 'look at this

social media and these articles on us, all of which legitimizes what we do.' It
gives new stores extra comfort in establishing a relationship with us."

While Panda's trajectory doesn't strictly follow the *direct response marketing* playbook, it certainly incorporates elements of it. For example, the company:

- Uses a compelling story,
- Collects personal data,
- Uses strategies such as social media to maintain contact and update its story, and
- Leverages the media to build credibility for both the story and the product.

Although Panda sells directly to the consumer from its website, it also relies heavily on developing relationships with retail outlets. As you can see, it entices prospective retailers to act quickly by making them aware that their competitors are already selling their sunglasses. They also have the data to back up their sales claims, which acts as further enticement (i.e., "By selling our product, you'll make more money—so why wait?").

Panda has shown there's room for innovation with direct response marketing and that pitching a credible offer in a way that compels action can be exceptionally effective.

Direct Mail is Alive and Well

As Bergeron and Lagera demonstrate, success depends on leveraging a mix of media and strategies. These include direct mail and radio *despite* the claims some make that they're dead. The fact is, nothing could be further from the truth. While you'll find cycles in which one spoke of the *Money Wheel* will work better than another,[73] these elements of direct response marketing have never and will never die out.

---

[73] Ergo the need to test, verify, and measure so you know which spokes are generating the highest return and why.

~~~~

"Six years after the launch of Facebook, North American consumers in the valued 18-34 year-old demographic prefer by a wide margin to learn about marketing offers via postal mail and newspapers rather than online sources ... "[74]

—Epsilon

~~~~

While I promote email as an important piece of many direct response marketing campaigns, direct mail plays an important role, too. Consider this: An email can be deleted instantly without the receiver ever reading the message. By contrast, direct mail requires receivers to walk from their mailbox to the recycle bin as they leaf through their mail. In that time, an effective direct mail piece can catch their eye, triggering the urge to open it and read the message inside.

For this reason, political campaigns rely heavily on direct mail—which is true even at the highest national electoral level. These expert campaigners understand that the walk from the mailbox to the recycling bin provides a critical opportunity for a direct-mail piece to take effect.

Is direct mail dead? Denny Hatch answers this way:

"Direct mail is very much alive. First off, the eighteen to thirty-four age group prefers direct mail to e-commerce. For one reason, these folks spend a lot of time online and are sick to death of spam. For another, with e-commerce, you the sender are one mouse click away from oblivion. Direct mail requires physical handling. You may open it over the trash can, but you must handle it. Third, a physical envelope—with screaming teasers— can be a lot more exciting than the little subject line in your inbox, which you could miss in a massive influx of spam. Fourth, direct mail is testable."

---

[74] Epsilon. "Young Adults Strongly Prefer Offline to Online Sources for Marketing Offers, Research Reveals." 2010. [Available from: http://www.epsilon.com/news-and-events/press-releases/2010/young-adults-strongly-prefer-offline-online-sources-marketing-offers]

This isn't meant to imply there's no place for e-commerce strategies such as email, social media, a web presence, and blogging. But it does show that direct mail remains an effective avenue during the *dating* phase.

Advertising on Radio

Also consider radio advertising. Fred Catona's story of developing a market for PriceLine.com should be enough to convince you that promotion in radio hasn't died. In fact, Catona dedicates his business to helping his clients market their products via radio advertising.

Is radio dead? Here's what Catona says:

> *"I have two responses to people who say radio is dead. The first is that the proof is in the pudding. I've made people millions and billions of dollars using it and still do every day, plus they're building brands with radio.*
>
> *"The second answer is more scientific. Radio has never changed. It occupies eight to nine percent of all budgets. Approximately ninety-three percent of all Americans listen to radio every week for seventeen hours. It's never changed and never will.*
>
> *"And radio and TV are the only two mediums that reach the whole population. Radio has ten thousand outlets with two hundred ninety-two million people a week listening to radio. That's a powerful medium."*

Radio offers another advantage: It can reach market segments by region and city, allowing you to tailor your message to the people you want to reach. This makes radio especially powerful and cost-effective marketing for entrepreneurs and small business owners who don't want or need a national presence.

~~~~

A recent Arbitron survey discovered approximately 93% of the U.S. population listens to radio during an average week. The reach has changed very little over the decades and remains a reliable entertainment and information source for listeners regardless of their demographic.[75]

—Arbitron

~~~~

---

[75] Arbitron. "Radio Today 2012: How America Listens to Radio: Executive Summary." 2012.

Recouping Your Dating Costs

As mentioned, the *dating* phase is the most expensive rung on the *ascension ladder*. You may have 100 suspects on your list, but only five may actually move ahead up the ladder and become customers or clients. Although this isn't a bad response rate, it means you've spent good money on the other 95 suspects. But keep in mind these 95 people may become prospects in the future. And they became suspects either because they were identified as being in your niche market or provided their emails or mailing addresses through an online form.[76]

Just because these prospects didn't respond to the first product or service you offered doesn't mean they won't respond to future offers. The breadth of factors makes it difficult to say why any one customer says yes and another no.

If you've shown these people different offerings in different ways from various angles and they've still said no, they probably aren't a good match. However, all may not be lost yet. You can take these 95 suspects and present them with offers from joint venture partners from whom you receive a commission. One of my clients did this with a group of suspects who didn't choose to do business with him, but he made well over $100,000 following up on affiliate endorsements in one month alone.

Always keep in mind the importance of referring these people only to offers of the highest quality and ones you believe in. Your endorsement needs to be authentic, or you risk losing credibility and trust.

From the *dating* stage of marketing, let's move into the *engagement* stage. You've wooed your suspects and turned some of them into prospects. Now what?

---

[76] Strategies exist to monetize the people who initially responded to your offer but didn't purchase. Believe it or not, one of the best ways is to work with your competitors to form a joint venture for non-converted leads. This is the type of discussions and insights we share as part of the Predictable Profits Insiders' Club. I know I'm biased, but if you've read this far in the book, I think you would find joining to be a wise decision. http://www.PredictableProfitsInsidersClub.com.

Chapter 8:
Engagement—Creating Enduring Loyalty

"Revolve your world around the customer and more
customers will revolve around you."
—Heather Williams

IF *DATING* REFERS to the art of gaining relationships, then *engagement* cements the relationship and builds loyalty. In this stage, you establish a communication routine that makes the customer or client feel acknowledged and appreciated.

Specifically, during *engagement,* you let buyers know you offer a unique solution and the best value. You ensure that they'll gain full value from your product or service so they come as close as possible to achieving the solution they sought. Here's an example of what I mean.

On the Predictable Profits website (PredictableProfits.com), I wrote a blog post titled *"The Dangers of Being 'Good' (and why it's okay to sleep with your customers!)"*. Yes, I wanted the headline to be provocative. But here's the point taken directly from my post:

That's right—I sleep with every one of my customers. I go to bed with men/women—hey, I don't discriminate—and I suggest you do as well.

I go to bed with every one of my customers on my mind and ask myself: "What can I do to provide my customers with a greater benefit and advantage to help them get closer to the ultimate result they are after?"

It's always about asking *The Growth Factor* question: *What more can I do to deliver the greatest value and experience, and what more can I do to help my customers or clients achieve the result they're after?*

Engagement begins with the initial purchase and proceeds as you move your customers from *liking* you to *loving* you. It's accomplished by providing ongoing exceptional service after the initial purchase by:

- Ensuring you receive their contact information,
- Following up to thank them for their purchase,
- Continuing to offer free value to ensure they gain the full value of their purchase (such as support, tips, newsletters, etc.), and
- Including periodic offers for additional products or services to help them achieve an even greater result.

Say you sell golf equipment. A customer buys a new driver hoping to increase the length and accuracy of his drives. Most of your competitors would let that person walk out the door without asking for contact information to follow up.

But what if you get the customer's contact information (often with the promise of additional free value)? You can send that person a thank you with instant access to free golf-swing clinic videos on a members' only webpage. Or email golf hints. Or ratings for local golf courses. Or messages with time-sensitive incentives for putters, golf balls, and related golf gear. These efforts will likely result in significantly greater loyalty, sales, and lifetime customer value. You can't lose.

Still, most entrepreneurs believe that, once the sale is made and the money's in the till, it's time to generate new customers or clients.

~~~~

An American Express survey found that 70% of American consumers were willing to spend more with brands that provided a great service, and a whopping 60% thought brands weren't thinking enough about the service experience.[77]

—TrendWatching.com

~~~~

If you understand the intent of the *engagement* phase, you realize your work truly begins when you acquire a new customer.

Customers or clients often look to you expectantly, waiting to see if you can continue to improve their lives and solve their deeper problem. They're almost always open to buying additional products or services that enhance the solution you've already sold them—if you've built a relationship with them. In that relationship, they continue to receive value and feel truly appreciated. When you do this, you'll gain much more than satisfied customers; you'll gain *ecstatic* buyers who'll return value to you. Not only will you benefit from additional, higher-value sales and escalating lifetime value; you'll receive their praise, referrals, and word-of-mouth recommendations.

Continuing with Direct Response

Direct response marketing carries as much importance in the *engagement* phase as in the *dating* phase. In fact, direct response marketing often works best with existing customers.

For example, working with one of my clients, we prepared a list of her *best customers*. We then created a marketing campaign that included two emails with a "preferred customer" offer including special pricing. We simply acknowledged their past business with us, extended our gratitude for their support, and provided them with a private and limited offer we believed they would like. With only two emails to her targeted list, she

---

[77] TrendWatching.com. Trend Briefing: "Servile Brands: Why for Brands, Serving, Assisting, and Lubricating is the New Selling." 2012. [Available from:
http://www.trendwatching.com/trends/pdf/2012-10%20SERVILE%20BRANDS.pdf]

achieved more sales in that single month than she did on that product all year. Sometimes, you simply have to ask for the sale.

Many small-business owners rarely go back to their existing clients and customers to make them a special offer. Instead, they're so busy trying to generate new ones, they neglect their current ones. Most assume they're already "hooked" and will come back automatically when they need something.

Many business owners also fail to appreciate that *New Consumers* have never had more choices and offers than today! It's not just the guy across town trying to steal your customers away; the World Wide Web is filled with businesses doing everything they can to poach from you. If you ignore your customers and fail to work hard at making them feel valued and appreciated, your business is vulnerable.

It's important to appreciate the voluntary aspect of a customer's relationship with you. Just as you'd never try to force someone into dating you, you can't force a prospect or customer to *engage* in a business relationship. As Kevin Hallenbeck says:

> *"Great sales people build a trusted relationship early. They clearly communicate that it's a voluntary relationship and, at any point, either can leave. Creating this freedom, offering real value, and building trust are critical components. If you're not willing to invest the time or money—or if you're not committed enough to do it—then it won't work.*
>
> *"So people have to commit to the process. This is why good salespeople enter into a dialogue, a conversation, with their customers."*

Some Only Like to Date

Do you understand that many consumers only like to *date*? This may be because they're price sensitive and only looking for the cheapest deal. In fact, according to Scott Hallman, a nationally recognized business growth trainer, only 14 percent of the buying public has price as their most important priority.[78]

---

[78] Hallman, S. "Total Impact Profit Report: A Service of Scott Hallman and The Small Business Growth Club." 2010.

Remember this: Those we seek to engage in a relationship want nothing more than to discover businesses *they never have to leave* because they feel valued and appreciated there. Researching new alternatives or competitors takes time and energy; your customers want to stay. And it's your job to keep them there.

Trust is Key to Any Relationship

When introducing the Edelman Trust Barometer earlier, I explained that significant majorities of the buying public don't trust or believe the claims made by businesses. By comparison, that means if you can earn their trust, *New Consumers* will gladly choose you to be their go-to person.

How do you build trust? Primarily through superior customer service and transparency. A recent survey by Oracle noted 20 percent of a company's average potential revenue loss stems from a poor customer experience. It also noted 97 percent of executives said improving customer service is critical to their success. And think about this: 89 percent of customers have said they switched to a competitor because of poor customer service while 86 percent of customers said improved customer service would encourage increased spending.[79]

According to research by LoyaltyOne, a global provider of relationship marketing services, "only 42% of respondents trust businesses. Nearly 75% of those consumers who do trust businesses are willing to provide more personal information in exchange for relevant offers and communications. Of those who don't trust businesses, only about half were willing to share their data."[80]

With the importance of customer service for building loyalty in mind, I read Gary Vaynerchuk's book *The Thank You Economy*. Vaynerchuk, known as "The King of Social Media," completely reinforces what I advise my clients, which is this:

---

[79] Oracle. *Oracle Customer Experience Global Survey, 2013.*
[http://www.oracle.com/us/solutions/customer-experience/oracle-customer-experience/overview/index.html]
[80] LoyaltyOne. "Consumers Question Benefit of Sharing Personal Info with Marketers." September 2012. [Available from: http://printinthemix.com/fastfacts/show/610]

"... The companies that will see the biggest returns won't be the ones that can throw the most money at an advertising campaign, but will be those that can prove they care about the customer more than anyone else."[81]

Customers demand authenticity, transparency, uniqueness, creativity, honesty and a genuine willingness to serve them at the highest level. As Vaynerchuk says, "The Internet has given consumers back their voice and tremendous power of their opinion via social media, which means that companies and brands have to compete on a whole different level than they used to."

Transparency, Authenticity, and Trust

Prospects, customers, and clients will trust you more if you're authentic and transparent. That means you have to openly demonstrate your desire to deliver the best possible experience. More than that, you show your commitment to helping them improve their lives and achieve their desires.

Jenn Lim, CEO and cofounder (with Tony Hsieh) of Delivering Happiness, echoes this point:

"When you think of developing customer loyalty and using customer service as a tool for that, it has to come from an authentic place or it feels forced. Recently, I read a blog post about a gentleman whose grandmother was dying in the hospital. She mentioned she'd love to eat a bowl of clam chowder from Panera Bread. This was on a Wednesday, and apparently Panera at this location only makes clam chowder on Fridays. The grandson called the manager and explained the situation, asking if there was any way he could get a bowl of clam chowder for his grandmother.

"The manager did what she needed to do and made a bowl of clam chowder. The grandmother and her grandson were thrilled. So the grandson tweets about it to say thanks, it goes viral, and Panera's Facebook page exploded with more than four hundred thousand 'likes' ... all because the manager got a bowl of clam chowder for granny.

---

[81] Vaynerchuk, Gary. *The Thank You Economy*. 2011: Harper Business.

"The blog post made the point that, back in the day, this level of customer service was normal.[82] *Does that mean we are so customer service deprived that getting a bowl of chowder for an elderly woman in the hospital creates this type of frenzy?"*

Lim also shares a contrasting story involving a realtor friend of hers.

"When I bought my first home, I called my friend and we stayed in touch for a while, but the relationship started to fade. For example, she now pays someone to send cards from her on Halloween, Thanksgiving, and Christmas. So when I wanted to sell my second house, even though I've already done multiple transactions with her, I didn't even think of calling her. Our relationship had gone from us talking all the time to getting automated cards, so it wasn't a real relationship anymore. It no longer felt authentic."

Both of these examples show the power of authenticity and transparency. They also indicate that simple acts of kindness have more impact than engineering a more complicated feat that's inauthentic. Clearly, making a bowl of clam chowder generated far more trust and loyalty than paying for someone to send a series of mass holiday mailings.

On a psychological level, people have many reasons they want and need to trust those with whom they do business. Primarily, they don't want to be taken advantage of and feel stupid. Rather, they want to feel smart—very smart—for having chosen to do business with you. Therefore, aim to help them feel smart.

The Power of Doing the Unexpected

What's the key to developing relationships in which your customers or clients love you? Do the unexpected for them. For example, my first multi-million-dollar business was a real estate development firm that produced

---

[82] This echoes a point in Vaynerchuk's book about the need customer service rarely seen since their great grandparents' day when business owners often knew the customers well and gave them personal attention.

high-end homes on a golf course in southern New Hampshire. My company handled nearly every detail of the home-building process—from design to site work to construction and beyond.

The process didn't end when the home was completed. I wanted to deliver an exceptional experience so my homebuyers felt appreciated. A piece of this included sending an unexpected gift. On the day families moved into their new homes, they were met with a giant custom basket of cookies and other goodies, plus a personal note thanking them for letting my company build their home.

This felt good to do, but it also acted as a psychological trigger. When you do something that's completely unexpected, people not only want to continue to do business with you, but they'll tell everyone they know about you.

I've been the recipient of a similar expression of gratitude. When my family, in-laws, and I went to the Cayman Islands for the first time, we ate out at a number of restaurants, trying a new one each night. Then we went to a recommended Italian restaurant. When we entered, I met the owner who was genuinely friendly and interested to learn about our family. Our conversation made for a wonderful welcome into her restaurant.

Throughout the meal, she periodically checked in to ask how we were enjoying ourselves. Then at the end of the meal, she brought everyone at the table a complimentary glass of limoncello, a lemon-flavored after-dinner liquor. After we complimented and thanked her, she mentioned it was made in the restaurant. Then she said since we liked the limoncello, she'd bring out samples of their desserts, which she did. Even though we'd passed on ordering desserts, we sampled them and found them delicious.

When we got back to the hotel, we told the concierge about our wonderful restaurant experience. The next day we went to the beach, then the pool, and then to the bar for a drink. At each place, we told everyone we met about our meal at that restaurant. My mother-in-law, who's a travel agent, even began recommending it to her clients when we got home.

So for the cost of house-made limoncello and a few dessert samples, the owner of this restaurant turned us into a word-of-mouth referral service for her business. Plus, not only did she benefit from our repeat business, the number of people we touched telling about the quality of our experience can't be counted.

Another unexpected event happened to Todd Niemaszyk from Atlantic Builders, a commercial and residential building company. While on a drive together, Todd told me he had to check on a job and invited me to do a walkthrough with him. Although he'd completed it more than a year earlier (and it was out of warranty), he was stopping by because the owner of the business had noticed two small areas of cracking. They were likely due to ordinary expansion and contraction attributed to seasonal changes.

When I saw the tiny cracks, I was surprised the business owner would call Niemaszyk and ask him to fix such a small problem out of warranty. But Todd corrected me, saying:

> *"The owner didn't call me. I told him I would be driving by his business and offered to take a look at anything that needed to be fixed. You see, people are so used to builders running away from problems that when I proactively call my clients to let them know I'm here for them, they're completely blown away."*

That's exactly why Todd's business has grown by several hundred percent over the last few years while many other tradesmen are struggling or going out of business.

Solid Customer Service Solidifies the Relationship

The way to continue engaging in relationships with customers varies from business to business. I spoke with Insiders' Club member, Nick Snyder of Digital Management Solutions, Inc., a provider of telecom solutions. He told me he realized soon after starting his company that his clients depended on reliability and service. However, they were often frustrated with the lack of service they received from the big telecom carriers. So Nick took it upon himself to create a full-service support team as a value-added benefit at no extra charge to his clients. Now, his team acts as the liaison between his clients and the big carriers to minimize his clients' frustrations.

The result? His clients have a much better telecommunications experience, and they love working with Nick's company. It has grown several hundred percent, quite an important distinction considering how heavily commoditized the telecom industry has become.

~~~~

RightNow Technologies reports that "55% of consumers recommend a company because of its customer service."[83]

—Oracle

~~~~

Remember Keith Lee, president of American Retail Supply? His company sells a wide range of retail store supplies and fixtures such as shopping bags, in-store displays, packaging, point-of-sale computer systems, price guns, and so on. If you recall, Keith—a quiet hero of customer service and innovation—is the one who wrote the 100-page book on customer service titled *Out-Nordstrom Nordstrom,* which he gives to clients.

Keith's exceptional customer service has made his company the leader in its industry. Here's one of his many stories:

"We have a 'Make You Happy Guarantee' with our point-of-sale computer systems. If you aren't happy with your system at any time within the first year, we'll refund your money and take the system back, no questions asked. One customer had owned a system for about a year and then wanted his money back. Quite frankly, we hadn't followed up on making sure he was happy. So we didn't realize he wasn't until he wanted his money back after a year.

"My sales rep said, 'Hey, this guy is messing with us. We shouldn't be giving him his money back.' Well, I didn't want to lose credibility on my money-back guarantee by not living up to it. So I refunded the money—about thirty thousand dollars—and back then, that was a ton of money for us. However, because we lived up to our guarantee, that customer has stayed with

---

[83] Oracle. *Oracle Customer Experience Global Survey, 2013.*

[http://www.oracle.com/us/solutions/customer-experience/oracle-customer-experience/overview/index.html]

us for the last twenty years and has bought over a million dollars' worth of our product.

"Not only that, but this customer happens to live in Juneau, Alaska, which is a close-knit retail environment, and he's told everybody about us. That was the best thirty grand I ever spent."

Again, be loyal to your customers or clients. Make them feel special and they'll be loyal to you.

Engage in Conversation With Your Customers

Elizabeth Marshall, a marketing strategist and coauthor of *The Contrarian Effect,* helps business authors craft and promote their books. She talks about listening to her client base this way:

"I have a brand with my cocreator Janet Goldstein called Book Breakthrough, which has been a three-day workshop for three years. Recently, we offered a four-week virtual edition because we listened to our audience. We were getting emails and feedback from people saying the New York City workshop looked great, but with their family vacation schedule and so on, they couldn't justify another trip away from home.

"So we became aware that our audience wanted something more accessible and mobile, given their personal schedules. It wasn't in our business plan to create a four-week virtual version, but we did it in response to these requests from our audience. We used the video footage from our 2011 workshop and, based on what we heard from our audience, broke it into nine lessons. These video classes are almost like TV broadcasts. We loaded them onto LiveStream and broadcast them at a certain time every day.

"The outcome for us was threefold. First, we got about eighty new people in our program. Second, we were able to help more people and make a difference in the lives of our customers and community. And third, this move led to bringing in many private clients.

"It became a game changer for us because, as entrepreneurs, we have great value and thought leadership, but we often see linear paths regarding how we can deliver what we know. The new approach provided an additional revenue

stream without having to create something from scratch. The point is, we were able to find and develop this new outlet because we listened."

You can't deliver greater-than-expected value to your customers if you don't know what they expect or the result they seek. This means constantly striving to understand their needs and desires is a critical component of your customer service program. If you recall, Walter Bergeron went to his customers and asked them what they wanted most from a company like his. As a result, he came up with the lifetime warranty for each piece of equipment he repairs. This type of communication led Keith Lee to come up with his "Make You Happy Guarantee." And this is how Ben McClure, owner of Gardner's Mattress & More, came up with his "Sleep Education" program for his customers.

If you keep the *The Growth Factor* question on your mind and take time to understand what your customers want, you *will* build loyalty in the *engagement* phase.

The How-to of the Engagement Phase

Let's talk about the tactics of the *engagement* phase and how you can bring specific methodologies to your own business.

Getting Your Customer Back in the Store

Fact: When customers or clients make a purchase—whether it's an initial purchase or their 20th—it gives you an incredible competitive advantage in winning their next purchase. They've done more than raise their hand to demonstrate interest. They're saying: *I want to do business with you, and you now have the opportunity to impress me with your product/service and exceed my expectations with your customer service.* They're also indicating they're interested in more.

The key to getting them back in your store or on your website and buying again is gathering as much information about them as possible. (At the very least, ask them for their name, email, and mailing address.) In fact, the more complete the information you keep on your buyers, the more you're able to make them feel valued. So ideally, you'll want to know their:

- Purchase history (including purchase details, amounts, and frequency),
- Preferences,
- Birthdays and important anniversaries, and
- Specific results they desire.

Then you can use all of this information to further personalize your communications.

~~~~

"The average business loses around 20 percent of its customers annually simply by failing to tend to customer relationships. In some industries this leakage is as high as 80 percent."[84]

—MarketingProfs

~~~~

As a side note, people seem to be far more comfortable giving a mailing address at the time of purchase than an email address. Giving away an email address has the perceived risk of receiving a deluge of spam. By contrast, giving away a mailing address feels less intrusive and requires the sender to make an effort to deliver the message.

GoTweets's *The Social Break-Up Report #8* says that, with email, "consumers want brands to send them relevant content that is tailored to their personal interests. They expect marketers to honor permissions and show restraint when it comes to email frequency. They measure your emails not against the best in your industry, but against the best senders in their inbox."[85]

---

[84] Jarski, V.M. "Customer Relationships: Breaking Up is Hard, Making Up is Harder." 2013. [Available from: http://www.marketingprofs.com/chirp/2013/10082/customer-relationships-breaking-up-is-hard-infographic]

[85] CoTweet. *The Social Break-Up Report #8.* 2011. [Available from: http://pages.exacttarget.com/SFF8-US?ls=Website&lss=Micro.SubscribersFansFollowersSocialBreakup&lssm=Corporate&camp=701A0000000NgyfIAC]

Be sure you record the specific product or service they've purchased. And, if possible, you want any other pertinent information that could indicate their preferences and desired result. Sometimes, you may want to give something free for all this information in the same way as you do during the *dating* phase. For example, at the checkout or time of service, you can ask for their name, mailing address, and email address with the offer of sending updates on new products and information on how to get more from the product or service they purchased. You can also print your website on the receipt and offer a discount on a future purchase for filling out a brief questionnaire on the website. Many retailers do this quite effectively.

When you capture their mailing addresses and other relevant information, you start to foster an initial relationship that becomes meaningful.

However, as mentioned, entrepreneurs and small business owners often neglect to collect this information. They believe that because their customers bought once, they'll continue to buy. They argue they don't want to be pushy or let people believe they'll receive endless promotions.

This is absolutely the wrong attitude to take. In today's global economy, you have more competition than ever in history. Companies and individuals all over the world are doing whatever they can to win the hearts of your customers and attract their next purchase. However, because you've already established that initial relationship, you have a competitive advantage over everybody else. Now you have to maintain that advantage via communication that feels comfortable *and* increases the value to those doing business with you.

This is the essence of being loyal to your customer.

To summarize, you want to establish an expectation of superior customer service shortly after the purchase. For example, there's a good chance when someone buys a product or service from one of my coaching clients or Insiders' Club Members, the new customer will receive a note, regular mail or email, within 48 hours that:

- Includes a thank you for choosing to do business with them,
- Reminds the recipient why he or she did business with them, and

- Offers a time-limited incentive to come back (e.g., a coupon, bonus item or a special price on a complementary product or service for first-time buyers).

The first two points establish doing business with your company as a friendly and pleasant experience; the third encourages them to come back soon. This helps get them in the habit of choosing *your* business over someone else's.

Don't Stop with a Thank You

Customer and client communication shouldn't end with a thank you. Rather, continue to lead them up the *ascension ladder*, building a relationship and maintaining their interest. These continued communications should follow the 80/20 rule. That means 80 percent of what you offer should add value to the initial purchase and help them get the result they're looking for; 20 percent should be valuable sales material, incentives, or offers.

Remember, a delicate balance exists between the information they want to read and any additional offers. For example, if you sell make-up supplies, you can offer periodic tips for following the latest trend with an offer and time-limited incentive to purchase products. These communications can take the form of:

- Newsletters,
- Occasional mailings with industry updates,
- New product announcements,
- Updates to current products, and/or
- Access to a members-only online community.

The only limits are your imagination and ability to innovate.

Establish a Methodology

Be sure to establish a set methodology for how and when you send out these communications—is it weekly, biweekly, or monthly? Are they sent via email, regular mail, or a combination of the two?

For example, if you own a paint store and someone makes an initial purchase, within 48 hours you'd send a thank-you note that includes an incentive to return. The second week, you'd send a newsletter on how to get the best results when painting various objects. The third week, you might send updates on new colors and types of paint or reminders that bathrooms need special mold-resistant paint. The fourth week, you could send a mailing with an email timed to arrive on the same day with a new offer and a time-limited enticement to buy. The fifth week's communication might include information on how to get the best painting result. Then back to the newsletter and so on. Oh, and by the way, most of this can be easily automated.[86]

Craig Simpson, the nation's leading direct-mail expert and founder of Simpson Direct, emphasizes it's all about bringing the customer into the family:

"Before starting my own consultancy, I worked for a financial publisher called the Ken Roberts Company, which educated more people on how to trade commodities than anyone else in the world at that time. We sold more than seven hundred thousand courses at one hundred ninety-five dollars apiece, and we did it one hundred percent through direct mail. Once they purchased the course, over the next seventeen weeks we made them eleven different offers, all through direct mail.

"One week, they got a promotional sales piece for another course similar to the commodities training course they'd already purchased. Maybe another week they got a sales piece promoting a stocks course that's financially related. The next week, they got a newsletter and the following week an offer to attend a live seminar. Then the week after, they may have received an offer for a video of the seminar with workbooks and such.

"So we sold seven hundred thousand people on the initial commodities course, but it didn't stop there. We had eleven other offers sent over the first seventeen weeks of being a customer with us. That kept them engaged and buying, which helped increase the customer lifetime value. We were making

---

[86] I've put together a list of automation tools for you at
http://www.PredictableProfitsPlaybook.com

five to six times the initial investment because we had a sophisticated customer retention path."

While I would argue this retention path was heavy on sales, it shows that significant additional value can be generated after an initial purchase. Although customer acquisition costs during the *dating* phase may be relatively high, during the *engagement* phase, you can generate greater profits by leveraging your competitive advantage with existing customers or clients.

Customer Retention Programs

Keith Lee is a proponent of establishing a customer retention program to increase loyalty, tighten customer relationships, and lead his customers along an ascension path. He states:

"We work at sending some value-add. One way is by sending our marketing tip of the week twice a week. More than twenty thousand retail stores get our tip of the week. It's designed to help retail stores do better marketing, customer service, management, etc. Typically, we include a sale item at the end of it to reward the people who read the tip. We figure they're closer to us and buy from us, and so we want to reward them.

"We send out a newsletter—ten thousand by snail mail and twenty-six thousand by email. The primary function of the newsletter is education. Sure, we put product in there, hoping we'll make some sales. If we break even with the newsletter production and the product advertised in it, that's good; but we do it for three reasons. One, to help our customers by giving them information to get them thinking about things they may have forgotten about and also to share new information. Two, to stay in front of them so they don't forget about us when it's time for them to order new products. And three, to sell something, but that's way down the line in importance.

"We get comments back all the time saying: love the newsletter, thanks for the marketing tips, nobody does this, thank you. That's key ... to make yourself unique from everyone else through what you do for your customers. You have to give them a reason to buy from you."

Failing to Follow Up is Like Failing to Care

Are you still leery about doing this level of follow up? Then consider what Craig Simpson says about his buying experience:

> *"I recently bought a brand new TV—a big flat screen—and I didn't go to Walmart to get it. I went to a place that sells high-quality TVs and electronics. Not that Walmart doesn't, but I wanted a place with a knowledgeable sales team so I could pick out the right television.*
>
> *"This was a classy store specializing in TVs and phones and cameras. When I bought the TV, I was expecting them to grab my name, address, and email because it seemed these guys had their act together. They're great on selling high-end merchandise, and I thought they'd follow up with me. Well, they didn't, and I was totally disappointed.*
>
> *"I was thinking they sure could've done a different job with me. Here I am, buying a brand new TV from a nice store; I'm affluent and willing to buy other stuff from them, so they should get me on their mailing list—but they don't have one."*

Certainly, the store owner could have leveraged Simpson's contact information to make repeated high-value offerings. As Simpson notes, he intentionally selected this store because it seemed like a *trusted authority*. During the purchase process, the store owner learned that Simpson's ultimate goal was a high-quality home entertainment experience, yet he didn't seek any contact information. This signaled to Simpson the store didn't have much interest in him. Additional sales could have been anything from new cables to connect the TV to video game consoles to BluRay players to stereo equipment—thus providing a total home sound solution.

The point is, the store had invested in advertising and marketing to convince Simpson it was a *trusted authority* in home entertainment, but the owner let that investment walk out the door after only one sale.

Up-, Down-, and Cross-selling

How can you increase the value of each sale as well as the lifetime value of each customer? Through *up-, down-,* and *cross-selling*. Of course, to be effective, these sales follow the guidelines presented so far. That means they:

- Relate to the original purchase,
- Reflect an understanding of what the customer or client seeks,
- Deliver the greatest value, advantage, benefit, and experience (e.g., *The Growth Factor*),
- Create and deliver on expectations of high customer service, and
- Follow the precepts of *direct response marketing*.

When these guidelines are followed, it's been my experience that as much as 64 percent of customers or clients will respond to a second offer within 48 hours of the initial sale. When making a second offer at the time of purchase, I've seen this rate go as high as 74 percent (the closer you make the offer to the original sale, the greater the result). This is where *up-, down-,* and *cross-selling* can be highly effective.

~~~~

"In a recent survey, only 37 percent [of business owners] said they use cross-sell and up-sell programs to boost revenue from existing customers."[87]

—MarketingProfs.com

~~~~

Up-selling

As it sounds, *up-selling* means offering consumers an enhanced product or service at the time of purchase. Perhaps the simplest example of an *up-sell* is when the local movie theater offers you extra-large popcorn for just a dollar more. I'm a marketing guy, and I laugh every time I reach into my pocket to hand over the money, knowing I'm falling for their *up-sell*. However, I don't want to run out of popcorn while watching a movie with my family. And I think *Hey—it's only a buck, so what the heck*. I may pay $8 for something that

---

[87] "Three Cross-Sell and Up-Sell Tactics to Boost Email Marketing ROI." 2012. [Available from: http://www.marketingprofs.com/short-articles/2668/three-cross-sell-and-up-sell-tactics-to-boost-email-marketing-roi]

costs a nickel to produce, but *I've already made that buying decision, so what's an-other dollar?* And that's how up-selling works.

Another example might involve buying a computer online. Manufacturers and retailers generally offer extra memory and other up-grades at the time of purchase. By adding value, this encourages buyers to increase their expenditures.

Car dealerships also excel at *up-selling*. They offer numerous additional features—car stereos, protective under-coatings, paint finishes, interior materials, and so on—to up the price and value of the car being purchased. And you've probably heard the ubiquitous fast food *up-sell*: "Do you want that supersized?"

Within the Predictable Profits methodology, *up-selling* is about helping people achieve a greater result while adding additional revenue to each sale at the time the sale is made.

Cross-selling

Cross-selling involves offers for products and services that are a little different from the original purchase but help the customer achieve a greater result. Often you communicate to the customer or client at the time of sale (or within about 48 hours) that, if you want a particular result, you may also be interested in this other product or service.

For example, when buying a computer from Apple, the company of-fers AppleCare, which is a suite of support services and products for the computer's hardware, software, and operating system. The price of AppleCare plans depends on the computer you're buying—last I checked it was $249 for a MacBook Pro, for example—to help customers get a better result from their new computer.

Another example is an insurance company offering to bundle home-owners and car insurance. Or an online prompt suggesting that, since you're interested in one product, you may also want to purchase these related products. Or travel sites offering to make hotel reservations when you book a flight. Or fast food employees asking, "Do you want fries with that?"

The *cross-sell* offers you another opportunity to deliver additional value to your buyers. You help them achieve the results they seek while increasing the lifetime value of that customer to you.

Down-selling

Down-selling generally occurs when the customer or client says no to the *up-* or *cross-sell*. In my AppleCare example, the company offers a premium service product designed to go beyond the customers' expectations for achieving the result they're after. However, not all buyers will dole out an additional $249, even if they believe they'd gain a lot from making that purchase. So Apple could offer AppleCare for one year instead of three and significantly reduce the price, saying that most issues arise in the first year. They could also drop certain services or products from the AppleCare premium suite and leave those most valuable to the consumer, reducing the price that way. In either instance, this shift represents a *down-sell*.

Car dealerships do this often, too. You may not want the high-end car sound system, so a scaled-down version is offered. Or when buying software, if you don't want the full version of a software product, the company generally provides a version with fewer features.

But it bears repeating that if you're *up-*, *cross-* and *down-selling*, never attempt to pitch a product just for the sake of making a sale. Only make offers that strictly connect to delivering a greater result. To do otherwise *decreases* the likelihood of repeat purchases and referrals and *increases* the likelihood of bad reviews.

Everything comes down to *The Growth Factor*. We live in a world where authenticity and transparency are becoming more and more important. The leaders in today's economy will head those organizations that people trust to deliver the best possible result they can.

Live Up to Their High Customer Service Expectations

As noted earlier, you want to establish an expectation for high customer service as early as possible, preferably in the *dating* phase. Then, during the *engagement* phase, you'd continually reinforce these expectations by living up to them.

For example, if you give a 365-day guarantee with free return shipping for your product, then you have to live up to it each and every time. There's a famous story of Nordstrom taking back a set of tires from a longstanding customer because the company wanted to live up to its guarantee. The kicker is Nordstrom doesn't sell tires!

Other legendary stories tell of L.L.Bean taking back boots years after they were sold. The store even took back an item 30 years after it was purchased.

Lands' End tells of a story whereby the wife of an avid car collector purchased a $19,000 vintage taxi featured on the cover of their holiday catalog and returned the used vehicle 21 years later for a full refund! They upheld their unconditional guarantee, which reads: "If you're not satisfied with any item, simply return it to us any time for an exchange or refund of its purchase price." Whatever. Whenever. Always.

It may be hard to dole out any refund money, but you can't beat the word of mouth that comes from ecstatically happy customers. Keith Lee knows this. That's why he creates big customer-service expectations as early as possible and then lives up to them, as he says:

> *"We sell to more than ten thousand retailers a year, and every one of them gets my direct phone line throughout the year. I put that direct phone line on hundreds of thousands of emails, snail mail newsletters, or other kinds of advertising. I want people to call immediately if we ever let them down, and if they're not satisfied, they can call me on my direct line.*
>
> *"One of the things that's highly important in 'out-Nordstrom Nordstrom customer service' is to be sure people understand the level of customer service to expect. If you tell them they should expect it all the time, then when they don't get it, they will tell you more often. In many other companies, when people get bad or indifferent customer service, they walk out and find somebody else. They don't say anything.*
>
> *"We love dissatisfied customers to call us so we can make things right. Most businesses, even if they're not practicing 'out-Nordstrom Nordstrom customer service,' probably want their customers to tell them when they mess up. The problem is most customers don't know the businesses want them to tell them.*
>
> *"So my phone number goes out hundreds of thousands of times a year. I get probably six to eight calls each year, and they always start with an apology such as, 'Keith, I saw in your message that if you ever let us down, we*

should call you, so that's why I'm calling.' And actually we get far, far more calls from people saying we're crazy good."

Sure, it may hurt to refund money in the short term, but the upside of doing so is far more powerful than the short-term loss. Strong guarantees also help bring in vastly more customers and income than without them.

Getting Full Value from Your Product or Service

Marginal entrepreneurs think all they have to do is make the sale and then move on. They actually don't spend much, if any, time thinking about whether people will ever use the product or information provided. Nor do they wonder or worry if they'll gain the maximum value from the product or service by using it properly. However, if you can help them get better results than they did before they met you, it's natural they'll want more from you. They'll also tell their friends about you. Remember, they want to look smart, so make it easy for them.

Therefore, the *engagement* phase calls for doing what you can to make sure your customers put your product or service to use—and do it correctly. You also want to follow up with good, actionable advice for how to gain the most value from your product or service. Plus, you need to fully understand the results your customers or clients seek.

Not only will this step ensure people feel ecstatic with their purchase, but it's part of your program of *engagement* to bring them back for additional purchases. For example, in your follow up, you can offer stories about how other customers have gained the full value of their purchase. Doing this is not only instructional, but it reminds them that others have had many positive experiences with your product or service. In essence, you're *reselling* the purchase to be sure they gain full value.

Again, if you're loyal to your customers, they will be loyal to you. Failing to do so will reduce referrals as well as the lifetime value of each customer. You'll also have an easier time getting them into the *marriage* phase—the most profitable of the three phases.

The Primary Tools of Engagement: Direct Mail and Email

The two most effective tools for following up with your customers for after-purchase support, product resell, and after-purchase marketing are email and direct mail. You can enhance the power of these two tools—especially in the case of email—by making them part of a coordinated campaign. In marketing terms, this refers to the complementary use of online and offline strategies.

Most *marginal entrepreneurs* (if they even capture email addresses) tend to use only email. Often, they believe it's cheaper than direct mail (which it is) and just as effective (which it isn't). For example, research by ExactTarget and CoTweet showed that 91 percent of consumers who subscribe to a company's email list unsubscribe soon afterward. Additionally, 77 percent of consumers say they're more cautious about giving companies their email address and another 18 percent say they never open email from companies.[88]

~~~~

According to Target Marketing Seventh Annual Media Usage Forecast Survey, "Direct mail is the channel cited most by B2C direct response marketers as delivering the strongest ROI for customer acquisition and retention."[89]

—Target Marketing

~~~~

Meanwhile, direct mail seems to be fairing quite well, having the highest rate of new-customer acquisition when compared to other marketing avenues. In one survey of marketing professionals, 34 percent of respond-

---

[88] CoTweet. *The Social Break-Up Report #8*. 2011. [Available from: http://pages.exacttarget.com/SFF8-US?ls=Website&lss=Micro.SubscribersFansFollowersSocialBreakup&lssm=Corporate&camp=701A0000000NgyfIAC]

[89] Target Marketing Seventh Annual Media Usage Forecast Survey. "Direct Mail Tips in ROI, Say B2C Marketers; Email Delivers for B2B." March 2013. [Available from: http://printinthemix.com/fastfacts/show/690]

ents gave direct mail the highest customer acquisition score; email came in second with 25 percent, search-engine marketing 10 percent, and affiliate marketing 8 percent. In addition, direct mail has the potential for significant ROI. One study found that advertisers spent an average of $167 per person on direct mail and earned $2,095 in sales. [90]

People also like to receive mail. Emails fly from every direction all day every day, but "snail mail" comes only six (soon maybe five) days a week in the U.S. A routine that's a hundred years old still carries the same sense of optimism with every trip to the mailbox. Therefore, a well-prepared direct mail piece has every chance of being read and its message received. Rather than having recipients simply hit delete, you have the time it takes them to walk from the mailbox to the recycling bin to get their attention—and once you have it, they will receive your message.

Combining direct mail with email is a powerful marketing tool. I work with coaching clients on timing so the direct mail and email arrive at times that complement each other *and* don't feel or look like junk mail or spam. Craig Simpson of Simpson Direct does much the same thing with his clients, as he says:

> *"It's not as if I send only direct mail to the customer. I email them, too. If today is Monday and I send out a mailing by first class mail, I have the same offer emailed to the customer on Wednesday or Thursday. I try to time it so the same day they get a piece from us in the mail, they're also getting an email.*
>
> *"It costs more to do direct mail, but the response rates are much higher with direct mail than email. Also, the people I work with go after a more affluent group, which is the fifty-plus crowd. This group still prefers direct mail over email, and they have the money to buy.*
>
> *"Plus we have a good chance of getting people to read our piece because we can be quite creative with our headlines and teaser copy on the envelope."*

---

[90] Young, M. "4 Direct Mail Statistics You Can't Ignore, in B&B: The More You Know." BB Log. November 11, 2012. . [Available from: http://themoreyouknowbandb.wordpress.com/2012/11/11/4-direct-mail-statistics-you-cant-ignore/]

Johnson & Murphy clothing mixes online and off-line by sending emails and coordinated direct mail with limited-time offers tailored to its customers' clothing needs. The company's pieces show an understanding that customers aren't ready to buy every day, but when the time comes, Johnson & Murphy (and its related brands) come to the buyers' minds.

From Engagement to Marriage

Dating creates the relationship; engagement solidifies the relationship and builds loyalty and value for both you and the customer. Next, in the *marriage* phase, customers or clients view you as more than a vendor or another business. They *rely* on you, regarding you as a partner in what they do— including buying the best shoes with the best customer service. Rather than thinking "where should I buy my next pair of shoes?" they only wonder what their next pair should be.

The same is true if you're a plumber or mattress salesman or software developer or financial services provider. You've gone from an unknown to someone who's provided an exceptional product or service, buying experience, and customer support and service. Therefore, your customers or clients become convinced that you're the right choice for whatever results they seek. That's the *marriage* phase, addressed in detail in the next chapter.

Chapter 9:
Marriage—The Mutual
Value Creation Engine

"A successful marriage requires falling in love many times,
always with the same person."
—Mignon McLaughlin, author

IN THE *MARRIAGE* phase, you bring your clients or customers up
the *ascension ladder* so far that they view you as essential in their lives. In their
eyes, you've become the unique provider of a solution for improvement.
After all, you've invested the money to acquire them and developed a relationship in which they trust you enough to keep spending with you. In this
phase, you continue the relationship by building on that trust and edging up
the lifetime value of those relationships.

~~~~

"If you don't take care of the customer, someone else will!"
—Raffaele Ciarla

~~~~

Why Marriage is the Most Profitable Phase

With the acquisition costs behind you, each subsequent purchase from a client or customer represents escalating profit. In my business—as well as that of my clients—I've found that it's six to eight times more costly to acquire a new customer than to lead an existing customer up the *ascension ladder* from *engagement* through to *marriage*. In fact, repeat business can account for between 30 and 80 percent of all profits.

~~~~

Customer acquisition costs include:

- Cost of advertising/promotion,
- New customer price sensitivity,
- Personal selling,
- Setting up new accounts,
- Time and money on explaining business,
- Cost associated with inefficient dealing with new customers.[91]

—E. Bloch

~~~~

Regarding the *marriage* phase of the sales process, customer retention specialist and president of New North Tobin Lehman wrote: "If the customer has a purchase history, then the cost of outreach you'll need to expend to invoke another purchase should be considerably less than the first-time acquisition cost. The customer has experienced the purchase process, you delivered on value, and they are using the product. Most of all the barriers to purchase have been crossed, so less capital is needed to influence the next purchase."[92]

---

[91] Bloch, E. "The Value of an Existing Customer." 2010. [Available from: http://www.flowtown.com/blog/the-value-of-an-existing-customer?display=wide]
[92] Lehman, T. *Kickstarting Your Customer Retention* ebook, 2013. [Available from: http://www.newnorth.com/ebook-kickstarting-customer-retention/]

With this increased trust and customer commitment, you can bring your buyers into higher-priced offerings. As a result, they're more open to up-sells and cross-sells at the time of purchase or shortly thereafter.

~~~~

Profits generated from satisfied customers:

- Reduced price sensitivity,
- Reduced switching to competitors,
- Increased referrals,
- Increased repeat purchases, and
- Increased number of customers and clients.[93]

—E. Bloch

~~~~

Remember, this does not negate the need for communication or mean you can stop asking *The Growth Factor* question. In fact, it's fundamental to continue bringing the customer up the *ascension ladder*.

Unfortunately, too many entrepreneurs and small-business owners drop the ball at this point. I recently spoke with a new Predictable Profits Insiders' Club member who works with businesses all over the world. He had a concern with repeat business and when I asked how often he communicates with his current customers, the response was "never." He believed his customers would contact him when necessary. *This is absolutely the wrong mindset.*

For Long-term Success, Develop Fanatical Customers

If Borders Books and Music had monitored the bigger picture (as we talked about in Chapter 2, "Look Comprehensively, Act Specifically") and been focused on how to deliver the greatest advantage to its customers, perhaps the company would still be in business. Borders made many mistakes when

---

[93] Bloch, E. "The Value of an Existing Customer," 2010. [Available from: http://www.flowtown.com/blog/the-value-of-an-existing-customer?display=wide]

the book and music industries went digital—an obvious market change they should have noticed. However, Borders continued to heavily invest in physical merchandise and relied almost exclusively on physical books and magazines for sales. The company failed to turn every buyer into a long-term, loyal customer by actively anticipating their needs as e-books and online purchases became more popular. Company principals believed the experience of being in one of their stores featuring a café was enough to entice people into getting into their car and driving there.[94] As analyst Rick Newman wrote: "The company made some poor decisions over the last decade and failed to adapt to new ways consumers shop and read books. It clung to an outdated strategy way too long and reacted slowly as more nimble competitors took its business away."[95]

Borders offers a prime example of what happens when customers are merely satisfied but not thrilled. Its customers began flocking to Amazon, Barnes & Noble, and iTunes to buy online.

Also consider Blockbuster, which at one time forced smaller, independently owned video rental stores out of business left and right. The basis of its success included a large selection and availability of videos—especially new releases—plus multiple convenient locations and no late fees.

However, Blockbuster took its eye off its customers and the problem the company solved for them. This retailer failed to maintain a comprehensive view of the competitive landscape and neglected to recognize that people wanted even greater selection and more convenience than it was offering. Therefore, when Netflix first came around, people left the brick-and-mortar rental stores for a more satisfying mail order experience. Blockbuster tried to play catch-up by offering its own mail order service—too late.

Then to put the final nail in the company's coffin, Netflix started streaming a huge selection of videos online and made it easy for people to

---

[94] "Beyond Borders: How the Failed Bookstore Chain Hastened its Demise." 2011. [Available from: http://www.cbsnews.com/8301-505124_162-42242498/beyond-borders-how-the-failed-bookstore-chain-hastened-its-demise/]

[95] Newman, R. "4 Lessons From the Demise of Borders Books." 2011. [Available from: http://www.usnews.com/news/blogs/rick-newman/2011/07/20/4-lessons-from-the-demise-of-borders]

access the service. Today, Netflix continues to evolve and stay loyal to its customers by making Netflix streaming even easier on new television sets and by investing $100 million to produce original programming.

In no small way, Blockbuster failed to provide its customers with the greatest advantage and lost them to a competitor offering better value. Netflix makes a deliberate effort to go above and beyond simple movie rentals to offer their customers an easy, convenient and pleasurable experience.

~~~~

"Litmus Test: If you are truly enriching someone's life, they will typically miss you in their past. They think their lives would have been even better if they had met you earlier."[96]

—Rajesh Setty, entrepreneur, author, speaker

~~~~

Now consider Walmart. Even the company's core customers don't expect anything other than a middling shopping experience. In fact, in a survey by the American Consumer Satisfaction Index, Walmart received the worst customer satisfaction score of all retailers as a result of customers disappointed with the store's customer service.[97]

By contrast, look at Apple, Zappos, and Amazon whose biggest assets include their respective raving customer bases. Another example is CrossFit. Its members are fanatical about this company that's loyal to them. CrossFit does everything it can to help them achieve their desired outcome. These perks include trainers for all members, nutritional guidance, and varied, individualized daily workout programs. In addition, the company works to build community among its members. As a result, CrossFit members are often jokingly labeled as a cult—and I'm proud to be a member of this cult.

---

[96] Gupta, S.G.I. "What Matters Now: Big Thoughts and Small Actions Make a Difference." Seth Godin's Blog. 2012. [Available from: http://sethgodin.typepad.com/files/what-matters-now-1.pdf]

[97] Hess, A.E.M. "9 Retailers with the Worst Customer Service." *USA Today.* March 16, 2013. [Available from: http://www.usatoday.com/story/money/business/2013/03/16/9-retailers-worst-customer-service/1991519/]

I love CrossFit because, even though it has more than 6,000 affiliated gyms, I feel as if it caters to my unique needs in achieving my fitness goals. And because so many of its members feel enthusiastic about the company, we go out and recruit others.

Consider Harley-Davidson. How many riders have the company's insignia tattooed on their bodies? How many Harley-Davidson bumper stickers do you see on everything from pickup trucks to BMWs to kids' bikes? A client of mine from many years ago even named his son Harley!

You may have heard the story of FedEx and the wedding dress, which has reached near-legend status.[98] When the company first started, it failed to catch on and hovered on the verge of bankruptcy for much of its early history. Then one day a frantic woman called to ask if FedEx could get her wedding dress from the east coast to the west coast by the next day. The company had trained its employees to go above and beyond for its customers, so—after running into some complications with the delivery—the company met its promise by chartering a private plane to personally fly the dress to the woman.

They didn't know the woman getting married was the daughter of Eastman Kodak, founder of the Kodak Company, and that she would rave about how this company saved her wedding at her reception. Of course, a number of corporate CEOs attended her wedding and heard this story of extraordinary customer service. Before long, FedEx had its first major corporate clients and went on to become what it is today.

I also point to JetBlue, which has ecstatic and incredibly loyal customers. Though it's known for being a low-price carrier, JetBlue has garnered a highly rated in-flight experience (e.g., no charge for the first checked bag, TV screens for each seat, and more). Almost always the first airline to provide assistance when the need arises, the company offers discounts to people traveling due to a tragedy. It also started a program to help families with autistic children.

---

[98] Kai-Lewis, K.S.E. "What can You Learn from this FedEx Story that Could Save Your Business from Going Under!" 2010. [Available from: http://new-billionaires.com/magazine/what-can-you-learn-from-this-fedex-story-that-could-save-your-business-from-going-under/]

What are simple, low-cost ways you can gain fanatical loyalty from your customers or clients?

Relationships Thrive with a Little Spice

"Affairs" happen in business. Most happen when customers feel they've been ignored or feel bored and want something new and exciting. Adopting the communication and customer service principles outlined in this book will go a long way to prevent a customer from feeling ignored.

That said, you can accomplish the communication and customer service aspects well, but if you aren't offering anything new to spice up the relationship, people can become bored and will disengage. Face it; people in our culture constantly seek the next best thing. They want to be first to introduce others to the next cutting-edge software, restaurant, consultant, house cleaner, accountant, insurer, or the like.

~~~~

"FOREVERISM: Encompasses the many ways that consumers and businesses are embracing conversations, relationships, and products that are never done. Driving its popularity is technology that allows them to find, follow, interact and collaborate forever with anyone & anything."[99]

—TrendWatching.com

~~~~

It feels good to find that "great new thing" and be the source for how friends and others find out about it.

To bring customers and clients up the *ascension ladder* to the *marriage* phase—as well as keep your current preferred ones happy—you have to spice up your relationships. Do something a little different to remind your customers how much you appreciate them. You'll edge up their loyalty that much more.

Remember, you always want to put something new or unique in front of them. It's like the Woody Allen line in which he says marriages are like

---

[99] TrendWatching.com. "Foreverism: Consumers and Businesses Embracing Conversations, Lifestyles and Products that are Never Done." 2009. [Available from: http://trendwatching.com/trends/foreverism/]

sharks; they always have to keep moving forward. In your business marriages, you want your customers to feel valued, to believe you're doing your best to help them achieve their desired goals. You can accomplish this by continually bringing fresh, compelling value to the relationship.

That requires applying your own creativity and ability to innovate while listening to your customers about their needs and desires. The following actions can spark your thinking about how to spice up your business marriages:

- Give preferred customers insider knowledge of a new product or service before the public and let them be the first to buy.
- Create complementary services to increase value of your product and the likelihood of a better outcome.
- Provide incentives or recognition to reward your customers for making additional purchases.
- Congratulate customer successes in your newsletters or email correspondence to those on your list.
- Seek opportunities to meet and/or socialize with your best customers.
- Randomly call your best customers to solicit one-on-one feedback and extend your appreciation.
- Send a thank-you gift after a repeat order.
- Customize communications and other interactions to each customer or client.
- Hold special, invitation-only customer appreciation events.

You may have noticed some overlap in the strategies used both in the *engagement* and *marriage* phases. The fact is, when you're dating someone, you send that person flowers to demonstrate your love and heighten his or her interest. After marriage, your wife or husband still enjoys these displays of love and affection.

Similarly, your customers still expect you to go above and beyond for them. Now, however, you need to find new ways to communicate the same message. You're still selling your customer on continuing to do business with you, but the idea of sending a dozen roses has grown old.

While I advocate going "above and beyond" expectations, even the little gestures can go a long way, as marketing strategist Elizabeth Marshall says:

> *"I proactively keep in touch with my higher-level, most committed clients. I may send members of my client family a relevant article. Or, if I notice them saying something on Twitter or I know they're working on a particular project, I'll send them a resource or article. And if I've worked with a particular client at that level, I might send an email to thank or congratulate that person. For example, one of my clients was just named a correspondent to CNBC, and I sent her a congratulations by email.*
>
> *"In these marriage-level relationships, when you deliver immense value they become referral engines for you. Right now, most of my private clients come exclusively from referrals, and I'm blessed to not have to work very hard to get new clients. I attract clients by delivering great service to the clients I have now."*

For Marshall, her gestures—large and small—have reduced the urgency to actively acquire new business. Although she still needs multiple spokes for her *money wheel*, she can count on many new customers coming to her through referrals.

Screwing Up: Finding Opportunity in Failure

A particularly surprising opportunity to create fanatical customers can stem from screwing up. No one sets out to intentionally make mistakes, but when you do, how you handle it can influence how customers or clients feel about your company. In fact, they can go from dissatisfied to fanatical.

~~~~

"The road to success is paved with well-handled mistakes."

—Neiman Marcus

~~~~

The best example of a well-handled mistake comes from Alex Wilcox, founder and CEO of JetSuite. Wilcox's company offers private jet transportation for corporate leaders and individuals traveling primarily in the western U.S. The company's *Unique Advantage Point* involves a low-cost, efficient alternative to commercial airlines for short-distance flights and acclaimed customer service.

Alex explains how a mistake became a great relationship-building opportunity:

> *"Human beings are flying in human-built airplanes up against the intricacies of Mother Nature. You combine people and machines and weather, and you have a recipe for inevitable delays.*
>
> *"So it's not if you will have delays, but how you react when they happen. Recently, we had an airplane flying with a customer from El Paso to Orange County in California—the CEO of one of the biggest natural gas companies in the country. While making a fuel stop in Albuquerque, the pilot had a technical problem with the airplane on the ground. It couldn't be repaired until the next day. The nearest airplane to recover that flight was three hours away.*
>
> *"Our customer services people were empowered to take care of this executive. So they secured him a hotel room and chauffeured car, and they instructed the hotel to ensure his breakfast the next day was portable so he could carry it on board. Then we got another crew to fly him the rest of the way the next morning.*
>
> *Although he was twelve hours late arriving in Orange County, the level of detail we put toward keeping him and his assistant informed while making sure everything was managed overcame the negative part of the experience. We arranged for one of our salespeople to meet him at the destination the next morning to apologize. A week and a half later, we got a letter from him thanking us for the way we handled the technical issue and the delay.*
>
> *"So this CEO paid ten to twelve times what it would have cost to fly commercially, and we delayed him by about twelve hours—but he thanked us. He now tells his friends how well we treated him."*

Wilcox and his staff took what could have been a relationship-ending experience and turned it into a moment of strength. I love that! This CEO not only feels ecstatic about the service and care he received, but it has strengthened his resolve to do business with JetSuite. He's even acting as an evangelist for JetSuite.

Keith Lee, president of American Retail Supply, shares another story of a company taking a tragic situation and turning it into an opportunity:

> *"We lost a distribution center in a fire in Denver. At the time, I believed we were fully insured for such an incident. However, we didn't have the insurance coverage we should have had.*
>
> *"Despite my partial responsibility in this, we received a check for $25,000 to cover at least part of what wasn't insured. We got it at a time when I was disappointed in the insurer and in myself that we didn't have the coverage we should have had. Then in walked the agent with a check for $25,000 out of his own pocket. It didn't come from the insurance company at all but from the agent himself.*
>
> *"I tell you, somebody would have to do a lot of work to get my business away from that agent."*

There's no lack of competition for Lee's business when it comes to his insurance coverage, but because of this one instance, a competitor would have to use dynamite to break up these two.

No, you won't always be perfect. Life just doesn't work that way. However, the way you handle screw-ups and acts of God can make the difference between a deflated customer perception of you and your company or a strengthening of the marriage.

Joint Ventures to Deliver Added Value

Joint ventures (JVs)—relationships formed with trusted vendors—can deliver a heightened experience to your customers or clients while creating mutual value.

When I was in my mid-20s and newly married, I formed JVs quite successfully with my real-estate company. As mentioned, we produced high-end homes on a beautiful piece of property on a golf course in southern New Hampshire. My company handled nearly every detail of the home-building process, from design to site work to construction.

Most people think that real estate developers sell and build homes and then move on to the next project. However, my wife Heather and I thought we could do more to add value to our clients' home-buying experience. We sat around our kitchen table and thought about all of the various products and services our homebuyers would need to create the perfect home.

This led to forming joint venture relationships with a wide range of companies: furniture, home theater equipment, driveway seal coating, landscaping design and maintenance, security systems, interior decoration, high-end lighting fixtures, and more.

We negotiated with these vendors to get preferred pricing for our clients and, along with the benefit these clients received, my company also received a percentage of the sales. Our reasoning was we'd already acquired the customer and would leverage our credibility to make these third-party offers to them. The costs of acquisition for the vendors was next to nothing—if not zero—while they were selling to a select group of high-end homebuyers.

This arrangement produced wins all the way around. We made additional profit from each sale while looking like heroes to our homebuyers. The homebuyers received preferred pricing on products and services they needed. And the vendors were able to grow their businesses among wealthy clientele.

Everybody won: our customers got better pricing, we made money, and the vendors acquired new customers.

In the end, this strategy added many, many thousands of dollars in revenue and gave us the honor of having one of the highest profit margins in the industry. I've also helped create JVs for my clients, which have increased their profits by as much as several million dollars over the course of a year.

Asking for Referrals

Earlier, you met Mike Michalowicz, noted business consultant, lecturer, and author. Before doing all of that, this entrepreneur made his first big breakthrough with his computer network integration company. He had niched his business to focus on hedge funds because he believed these people were the hungriest for his offer.

Mike describes how he kept growing his business this way:

> *"It's common to ask clients for referrals, but it always feels uncomfortable to me. They've just given me a big check and now I want them to refer me to their friends, their family, their first of kin. So effectively, I'm saying thanks for the check, but now you have to give away your relationships to me.*
>
> *"Instead, I ask about other vendors. So I went to Larry, one of my first hedge fund clients, and said, 'Hey, I know you've been working with me for a year or more. Could you tell me about other vendors you use? Not my competition but vendors used for services such as your cleaning company?'*
>
> *"I told him if I understood what his other vendors were doing, I could contact those people, tell them what services I'm providing for him, and collaborate to collectively service him better. He gave me his list of vendors and pointed out his three favorite. I called those vendors, saying we had a mutual client we were servicing. I suggested getting together for a cup of coffee and discuss how we could complement each other. One of these guys owned a cleaning company. We discovered ways to make each of us more efficient. That made both Larry and the other vendor happier because we found ways to make their lives easier.*
>
> *"Then the miracle moment came. When I went back to the cleaning company a month later saying he was working out well, I asked if he worked with any other hedge funds. He replied, 'Oh my god yes; we have a certain security clearance that allows us to work in places in the financial industry and financial trading.' So I asked if, since we were working well together, he would refer me to those clients. Knowing they often had problems with computer guys, he said yes. I built similar relationships with even more vendors, and within two years, I brought in seventy new hedge funds clients. After that, my company exploded."*

I might add that Michalowicz could have used these relationships to also create a new profit center by receiving a referral fee or a share of the profits through his endorsement. And he could further serve his clients by negotiating a preferred customer discount from the vendor.

You could follow suit after asking these questions:

- Who are my customers doing business with both before working with me and simultaneously? This identifies potential partners who could refer business to you in exchange for a referral fee.
- What different things are my customers acquiring or going to need after they do business with me? You can negotiate preferential pricing for your client and collect a referral fee and/or share in the profits.
- What different things could further improve my clients' lives or help them get closer to the result they're after?

After identifying who has these various products or services, reach out to them. It's critical to vet these potential partners through interviews and references. They can't be considered only *good* vendors; they have to be *great* vendors.

As a cautionary note, Alex Wilcox of JetSuite tells the following story to demonstrate the importance of endorsing only those who will deliver the highest quality:

"We don't offer meals on our planes, but when someone wanted catering, we referred them to a company that could provide it. However, we removed ourselves from that loop. We realized that, due to a few factors we can't control, it's outside our core competency.

"We learned this the hard way. One time a client flying to a Lakers pro basketball game wanted food and desserts in his team's colors, which are purple and gold. He ended up getting cupcakes with green frosting. Of course, the Lakers were playing the Celtics that night, and that team's color is green.

"So this customer ended up hating us. We literally lost him because we delivered the wrong color frosting on a cupcake. This guy worth two hundred and fifty thousand a year to us was lost as a customer due to twelve cents worth of food coloring."

Once you've vetted a potential vendor, negotiate for preferred pricing and a referral fee. Be sure to point out that you've already spent the money to acquire the customer. Also convey that you've built a significant degree of trust, authenticity, and reputation with your customers—factors that will dramatically increase the conversion rate. These reduced costs, your time and reputation, and probable conversion will mean increased profits for the right vendor—a win-win for the two of you and for your customers.

Winning Back a Disengaged Customer

No matter how good you are, you'll have marriage-phase customers who become disengaged. As noted earlier, most "affairs" occur because the communication channel breaks down and the customer feels ignored or someone in your company did something that left the customer feeling dissatisfied.

However, "affairs" also happen because life gets in the way—customers move, get sick, or alter their buying pattern for a myriad of reasons. This commonly happens to clients of dentists, as an example, so most dental offices call or email appointment reminders to their clients to reduce the number of missed appointments. Have you been in the routine of getting regular dental cleanings every six months, only to have a work or family obligation get in the way? The next thing you know, it's been eight months or a year since your last exam. In this case, the dentist's strategy should be, and often is, to send a gentle pre-appointment reminder.

~~~~

"When you recognize that over 80% of all lost clients didn't leave for an irreparable reason, you can instantly take action and get many—even most—of those clients back. And when they do come back, they tend to become one of your best, most frequent and loyal client groups."[100]

—Jay Abraham, CEO of the Abraham Group, Inc.

~~~~

---

[100] Abraham, J. *Getting Everything You Can Out of All You Got: 21 Ways You can Out-Think, Out-Perform, and Out-Earn the Competition.* 2001: St. Martin's Griffin. P. 28.

When my family and I moved to a nearby town on the New Hampshire seacoast, our move disrupted what I presumed was an important customer relationship. You see, my wife has a fear of spiders, so for more than three years we had a pest-control company come out once a month to clear out the spiders.

With moving, we fell out of the buying pattern with this company. Its owner didn't reach out to see what had happened or offer us service at the new address. Eventually, I saw a flyer for pest control from a different company offering what seemed like a good deal, so this company got my business.

Many service businesses fail to do follow-up. Carpet cleaners could educate their clients on why regular cleanings are healthy and helpful, and then send out reminders at regular intervals. They could also tailor their messaging to each customer's circumstances, mentioning young kids, pets, older home, and so on.

Hair salons rely on customers to know when they need to have their hair done or any other salon services. But by collecting contact information, they can keep patrons up to date with new services and special time-limited offers to build loyalty.

Even large-equipment repair specialists can keep in touch with clients and send out reminders for routine maintenance, notice of new services, special rates, and time-limited offers. They could be offers to loyal customers as well as information on their particular type of equipment.

Think about what you could do to improve your *marriage-phase* relationships and ensure your customers or client don't have "affairs" with others. And if they do wander off, have specific strategies to win them back.

Ask Why They Left

As an entrepreneur or small-business owner, it's your responsibility to find out why customers have disengaged, and then deploy what I call *The Customer ReEngagement Strategy*.[101]

---

[101] For a templates and a step-by-step guide on employing *The Customer ReEngagement Strategy*, visit http://www.CustomerReEngagement.com

I have my clients look at their disengaged customers and reach out with a communication that acknowledges their departure. It says they're aware they haven't heard from them in some time, and they express genuine concern. They also ask if there's anything the company may have done to cause them to stop doing business, saying *please let us know so we can do whatever it takes to make it right.*

Sometimes they offer disengaged customers a time-limited enticement to get them to come back, such as a preferred customer discount, limited offer, or anything they think might get them back into the buying cycle. Simply by deploying customer re-engagement strategies like these, my clients have seen as much as a 100-percent increase in sales within 14 days.

In one case, my client sent out the re-engagement communication to her customers on a Monday. When I didn't hear back about the response, I called and got no answer, which had me worried. Then a few days later when I finally reached her, she said, "Charlie, I'm so sorry I haven't been in touch, but I'm just swamped. This is the first time we've tried anything like this, and I have to tell you, my assistant and I have been up twenty-four hours because we've received so many notes from our customers saying 'thank you so much for the acknowledging me' that I felt the need to personally respond to each one of them."

To say the least, this one communication resulted in a significant increase in sales, re-engaged many of her customers, and helped lead them further up the *ascension ladder.*

Then there's Keith Lee, whom I highly regard when it comes to customer service. He intends to reach a time when his customers see him and his company as an unpaid employee, as he describes when he first went out into the field as a sales rep:

> *"We sold handheld price-marking guns way back in the 1970s when it was ka-chik label, ka-chik label, and so on. My job was to go around to retail stores that had bought from us in the past and get them to buy from us again.*
>
> *"Well most of them had gone to some other vendor because someone else was walking in and taking their orders. I'd go into the stores and walk around, trying not to see anybody right away so I could look at the labels on*

their products. I tried to find labels that didn't look good, that weren't print-ing properly.

"Then I'd go up to whomever was in charge and say, 'I'm Keith Lee with Thompson Marking Service, and I'm here to service your price-marking guns.' That person would say, 'We don't buy from you anymore because somebody else came around.'

I'd reply, 'That's alright; I'll just lubricate them, service them, and make sure they're working okay.'

"'Well, we don't buy from you anymore,' the manager would say again.

"Then I'd show him a label or three that weren't printed right and say, 'You see these labels? I can fix that problem for you if you want while I'm here. Would it be okay if I take a look at your print gun?' And he'd say sure. So I'd fix it and get it so it printed properly and show him what I did and he'd thank me. 'I'll be back in a few months,' I'd say. He'd repeat that they don't buy from us, and I'd say, 'Don't worry about it.' Then I'd come back in a few months and do the same thing.

"When they saw I fixed their price marking guns, a number of them would give me an order. Others would say we don't buy from you anymore and off I'd go. I'd come back two or three months later, do the same thing, and pick up more orders. Some of them would still say we don't buy from you anymore, but I kept doing that. Soon, I had won back almost every single customer.

"That's the whole idea of becoming an unpaid employee. Nobody was fixing those price guns for them; I was doing something they would have had to train somebody else to do. So the whole idea is to become an unpaid employee—someone they'd say did a huge service for us."

I love this story because it shows how a little innovation can go a long way. It also highlights an important piece of all marketing—that is, you can't overestimate the importance of making somebody feel special, valued, appreciated, and acknowledged. These are incredibly important factors in human and business relationships, which to me are one and the same. It's people doing business with people because they know, like, and respect each other. This kind of mutually beneficial relationship makes for a successful *marriage* phase.

Parting Thoughts

"If I had nine hours to chop down a tree,
I'd spend the first six sharpening my ax."

—Abraham Lincoln

MUCH OF THE advice in this book points to positioning yourself as a trusted authority, creating a greater advantage for your customers, and making your customers or clients feel valued, special, acknowledged, and appreciated. Yet people ask me, *What does that have to do with marketing?*

Marketing today applies to *any activity related to buying and keeping your customers.* And by following the principles in this book, you ensure that people in your market don't view your product or service as another commodity. If you allow that to happen, then you're nothing more than a salesperson with a self-interested agenda. And if you're set up to compete on price, you won't ever earn loyalty from your customers.

With China producing products at an exceptionally cheap price and India operating with criminally low labor costs, know this: *You'll always have competitors offering cheaper products and services than you do.* Just ask Walmart. That's why the primary objective of Predictable Profits methodology requires transcending the *commodity perception* and becoming viewed as the *provider of a valuable and unique solution*—that is, being a strategic entrepreneur.

It's time to take low pricing out of the decision-making equation. Add value and focus on relationship building to make your company not only the *obvious* choice but the *most desirable* choice.

So there you have it. You've received lessons from brilliant business minds—ones who've been dominating large enterprises as well as dozens of small business owners carving their way to the top. You now have *Positioning* strategies for becoming the notable go-to company in your market, *Product* strategies for building the foundation of your growing empire, and *Promotion* strategies for out-thinking, out-maneuvering, out-earning, and out-marketing your competition.

It starts with a single step and a commitment to consistency. Stay on track, and you'll join the ranks of those enjoying a solid, recession-proof business.

Be the best you can be in your endeavors as a strategic entrepreneur. I'm here to help.

About the Author

Charles E. Gaudet II is the CEO of Predictable Profits, a leading marketing, coaching, and consulting company specializing in helping small businesses grow and become leaders in their markets.

Charlie has been an entrepreneur since the young age of four when he sold artwork to his neighbors. Year after year, his entrepreneurial journey gained traction. His business ventures ranged from establishing a bathroom tollbooth at his parents' home (which they shockingly agreed to play along with) to creating an angel-financed pet health insurance company (which was nominated *"One of the Nation's Best Seed-Stage Companies"* by accounting giant Ernst & Young) to a multimillion-dollar real estate development company—and many others.

Today, Charlie's advice has appeared in media throughout the world including Fox Business, Inc., *Forbes,* and *Business Insider*, plus he has spoken to both domestic and international audiences. He was selected as one of

The American Genius Beat's "Top 50 Influencers." On occasion, his kids even take his advice.

Charlie is a three-time wrestling state champion, an avid CrossFit athlete and competitor, and a wake boarder. To feed his ravenous appetite for quality entrepreneurial and personal achievement information, he has invested more than $500,000 studying thought-leaders, billionaires, multimillionaires, entrepreneurs, celebrities, and leaders of all types.

A member of the Young Entrepreneur's Council and an alumnus of Babson College, he lives in Portsmouth, New Hampshire, with his wife, three children, and their 120-pound lap dog.

Nobody has ever called Charlie "ordinary."

Acknowledgments

My thanks to all the amazing folks whose thoughts are featured throughout this book: Jay Abraham, Walter Bergeron, Bill Bonner, Bob Bly, Fred Catona, Ronald Drozdenko, Ph.D., Julia Erickson, Jeff Giagnocavo, Greg Habstritt, Kevin Hallenbeck, Paul Hartunian, Denny Hatch, Anne Holland, Aaron Ingley, Luke Lagera, Jenn Lee, Keith Lee, Paul Lemberg, Jenn Lim, Mike Michalowicz, Ben McClure, Nate Moss, Todd Niemaszyk, Sarah Robinson, Rich Schefren, Craig Simpson, Nick Snyder, Siamak Taghaddos, Marshall Thurber, Tom Trush, and Alex Wilcox.

In addition to these contributors, this book wouldn't exist if it weren't for the ingenious wisdom imparted by numerous entrepreneurs and thought leaders—some of whom I have met, many of whom I have simply studied. These include Jeff Bezos, Drayton Bird, Sir Richard Branson, Warren Buffett, Andrew Carnegie, Robert Cialdini, Robert Collier, Dr. John DeMartini, Walt Disney, Peter Drucker, Buckminster Fuller, Seth Godin, Gary Halbert, Claude Hopkins, Dan Kennedy, Bill Kelleher, Tony Hsieh, Steve Jobs, David Ogilvy, Tony Robbins, Howard Schultz, Fred W. Smith, and dozens more.

I also thank my Insiders' Club members as well as my Platinum Business Coaching Members and Centurion-level clients. They inspire me every day. While it might sound crazy coming out of the mouth of a business guy, I really do *love* the people I work with. After all, *together we are better!*

Thank you to my editors Emily Loose, Barbara McNichol, and my wife, Heather Gaudet, for pushing me to make this book better than ever. I also extend my warm appreciation to James Buchanan who has been my right-hand man during this creation, dedicating hundreds of hours to make it happen.

It would be absolutely insane to leave out my "rock star" assistant Mike Schertenlieb. If I'm the train, Mike is the rails keeping me on track, on task, and highly focused. I am blessed and grateful to have Mike as my right-hand man.

To my friends (you know exactly who you are): Thanks for being there as shoulders to lean on and a wonderful source of fun, laughter, and good times.

To my "6am'ers" and the entire Crossfit Portsmouth family: Thank you for all the encouragement, laughter and positivity you bring me each and every day.

To my parents Louise and Charles: Thanks for never allowing me to be okay with mediocrity, always pushing me to be my best. Your love and ongoing support—as well as the comfort of knowing I can <u>always</u> rely on you—has meant more to me than words can describe.

To my brothers Chris and Jon-Ross and their respective spouses Ting and Sara, and to my sister Jolie: Thanks for all the adventures we've had and the memories we've yet to create. It's nice to know you feel as proud of me as I do of you. To my nephew, Christopher, and my niece, Waverly, I'm very, very proud to be your uncle.

To my in-laws Ken, Linda, and Jason: Thanks for welcoming me into your family and being okay with letting me take Heather on this crazy rollercoaster ride called "entrepreneurship."

To my wife Heather: Where do I begin? This book could easily double in size if I were to list every reason you have made me a better person, entrepreneur, husband, and father. When I've fallen, you've picked me up. When I'm celebrating, you're by my side. There's not a soul on this planet who has touched my life and my heart more profoundly than you, Heather. It's been said that behind every man there's a better woman. Well, in my case, this couldn't be more true. Not only beautiful on the outside, you are stunningly beautiful and brilliant on the inside.

And to our kids Branson, Sage, and Sabrina: This book is really for <u>you</u>. You are my life, my inspiration. If I could teach you half of what you've already taught me, my life would be complete.

Index

Business Accelerators
Action Steps for Dominating your Market

1. Access the <u>FREE</u> Book-Owners' Exclusive Members Area
Register to get instant access to <u>FREE</u> additional and private resources just for you at:
http://www.PredictableProfitsPlaybook.com

2. Read the Predictable Profits Blog
Tap into the latest discussion and receive tips for maximizing your business growth at:
http://www.PredictableProfits.com/blog

3. Sign Up for the <u>FREE</u> Predictable Profits Weekly Newsletter
Get free marketing tips and more by registering for our weekly newsletter at:
http://www.PredictableProfits.com/newsletter

4. Follow Us!
Join the conversation and connect with Charlie at:
http://Facebook.com/PredictableProfits
http://Twitter.com/CharlesGaudet
http://www.linkedin.com/in/charlesgaudet/
http://google.com/+CharlesGaudetII

5. When Entrepreneurs Are Serious About Creating Predictable Profits, This Is What They Do …

The Predictable Profits Insiders' Club offers determined entrepreneurs like you the opportunity to discover advanced trends, strategies and ideas for growing your business.

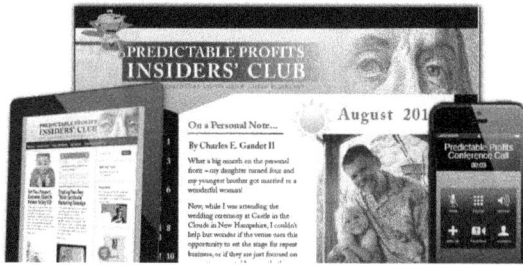

This limited-invitation membership is designed to help you implement the knowledge you gained from this book and dive deeper into the strategies you need to accelerate Predictable Profits inside your business.

And there is no better time than now to be an Insider.

Here's why:

1. You will see how to find hidden profit-building opportunities your competition overlooks!

2. In a bad economy, your competition is weak (so winning is easy)!

3. When times get tough, your competition becomes paralyzed with fear (playing the blame game on the government, economy and other factors outside their control), while you will have access to tools and resources that create steady growth!

4. While your competition wastes money on marketing methods that fail, you will discover how to intelligently re-invest in what works)!

5. Your competition believes they must compete on price to get the sale, creating lower profit margins (while you will learn methods for getting premium pricing so you can out-market, out-maneuver and out-earn your competition)!

But that's just the beginning. Get complete details on the Predictable Profits Insiders' Club and check for openings today at

http://www.JointheInsidersClub.com